Affordable Houses Designed By Architects

Architectural Record Books

Apartments, Townhouses and
    Condominiums, 2/e
The Architectural Record Book of Vacation
    Houses, 2/e
Buildings for Commerce and Industry
Buildings for the Arts
Campus Planning and Design
Great Houses for View Sites, Beach Sites, Sites
    in the Woods, Meadow Sites, Small Sites,
    Sloping Sites, Steep Sites, and Flat Sites
Hospitals and Health Care Facilities, 2/e
Houses Architects Design for Themselves
Houses of the West
Interior Spaces Designed by Architects
Office Building Design, 2/e
Places for People: Hotels, Motels, Restaurants,
    Bars, Clubs, Community Recreation
    Facilities, Camps, Parks, Plazas,
    Playgrounds
Recycling Buildings: Renovations,
    Remodelings, Restorations, and Reuses
Techniques of Successful Practice, 2/e
A Treasury of Contemporary Houses

Architectural Record Series Books

Ayers: Specifications for Architecture,
    Engineering and Construction
Feldman: Building Design for Maintainability
Heery: Time, Cost, and Architecture
Heimsath: Behavioral Architecture
Hopf: Designer's Guide to OSHA
Portman and Barnett: The Architect as
    Developer
Redstone: The New Downtowns

Affordable Houses Designed By Architects

EDITED BY JEREMY ROBINSON

An Architectural Record Book
McGraw-Hill Book Company

New York	St. Louis	San Francisco	Auckland
Bogotá	Düsseldorf	Johannesburg	London
Madrid	Mexico	Montreal	New Delhi
Panama	Paris	São Paulo	Singapore
Sydney	Tokyo	Toronto	

The editors for this book were
Tyler G. Hicks and Sue Cymes.

The designer was Irving Weksler.

The production supervisors were
Elizabeth Dineen and Tom Kowalczyk.

Printed and bound by Halliday
Lithograph Corporation.

Library of Congress Cataloging
in Publication Data
Main entry under title:

Affordable houses designed by architects.

    "An Architectural record book."
    Includes index.
    1. Architect-designed houses — Prices.
 I. Robinson, Jeremy, 1940-
 II. Architectural record.
 NA7125.A35   728.3   78-11471
 ISBN 0-07-002341-7

 567890   HDHD   7876

Table of Contents

Introduction VIII

Chapter One:
INGENIOUS SOLUTIONS X
  McKim Residence, San Diego, California   2
  Holmes Residence, Tampa, Florida   4
  Cannady Residence, Houston, Texas   6
  Shafer Residence, Annandale-on-Hudson,
    New York   8
  Riley Residence, Inverness, California 12
  Lipman Residence, Denver, Colorado 14
  Traverso Residence, Westbrook, Connecticut . . 16
  Schwarz Residence, Mill Valley, California 18

Chapter Two:
HEIRS TO THE INDUSTRIAL REVOLUTION **20**
  Burke Residence, Watermill, New York 22
  Bruder Residence, New River, Arizona 24
  Gueron Residence, East Hampton, New York . . 26
  Bohlin Residence, West Cornwall,
    Connecticut 28
  Tollefson Residence, Wausa, Nebraska 32
  Brandzel Residence, Fremont, Nebraska 34
  Van der Ryn Residence, Point Reyes,
    California 36

Chapter Three:
SNUG RETREATS **38**
  Crossman Residence, Sea Ranch,
    Sonoma County, California 40
  DeVido Residence, East Hampton, New York . . . 41
  Lovett Residence, Crane Island, Washington . . 44
  Dunbar Residence, Winhall, Vermont 46
  Kindorf Residence, Plumas County,
    California 50
  Daland Residence, West Bethel, Maine 52

Chapter Four:
SITE DETERMINED SOLUTIONS **54**
  Leader Residence, Sag Harbor, New York 56
  Mark Residence, Truro, Massachusetts 58

Chapter Four: (continued)

Chiu Residence, Vancouver,
British Columbia 60
Maxey Residence, Wayne County,
Pennsylvania 62
Canavan Residence, Hanover,
New Hampshire 64
Karas Residence, Berkeley, California 67
Campbell Residence, Sausalito, California 70
Fowler Residence, Houston, Texas 74

Chapter Five:
HOUSES AS SCULPTURE **76**
Frankel Residence, Margate, New Jersey 78
Lowenstein Residence, Montauk, Long Island . . 80
DeSwaan Residence, Bridgehampton,
Long Island 82
Moger Residence, Southampton, New York 84
Ballentine Residence, Atlantic Beach, Florida . . 86
Weinberger Residence, Miami, Florida 88
Private Residence, northwestern Illinois 90

Chapter Six:
WITH A VIEW IN MIND **92**
Private Residence, Des Moines, Iowa 94
Whisnant Residence, Charlotte,
North Carolina 96
Meilleur Residence, Bellevue, Washington 98
LeBovit Residence, McLean, Virginia 100
Adams Residence, Roseau, Minnesota 102
Curry Residence, Montauk Point, Long Island . . 104

Chapter Seven:
RENOVATION AND RECYCLING 106
   Christiansen Residence, Frog Hollow,
     Michigan 108
   Private Residence, Nyack, New York 110
   Opp Residence, St. Paul, Minnesota 112
   Desburg Residence, central Ohio 114
   Kimball Residence, Andover, Massachusetts . . 116
   Private Residence, Bedford, New York 120

Chapter Eight:
BRINGING THE OUTDOORS INDOORS—
AND VICE VERSA 124
   Riley Residence, Guilford, Connecticut 126
   Hall Residence, Napa, California 128
   Hobbs Residence, Seattle, Washington 132
   Lam Residence, Cotuit, Massachusetts 134
   Woo Residence, Los Angeles, California 136
   Schmidt Residence, Coconut Grove, Florida . . . 140
   Glass Residence, Des Moines, Iowa 142
   Grey Residence, Wellfleet, Massachusetts 146
   Benenson Residence, Hawley, Pennsylvania . . 148

Chapter Nine:
IN THE CLASSIC MANNER 152
   Freidin Residence, Weston, Connecticut 154
   Grossman Residence, Parker, Colorado 156
   Hickman Residence, Lakeside, Michigan 158
   Sorey Residence, Oklahoma City, Oklahoma . . 160
   Ernest Residence, Atlantic Beach, Florida 162

Index 166

Affordable Houses Designed by Architects

Introduction

Would you like to own a home designed by an architect for you and your family? The answer most people would come up with is, "Yes, but I can't afford it." The 62 houses in this book may change your mind about the second part of that statement, but right now let's look at the reasons why most of us respond to that question with a qualified 'yes.'

At one time or another you've been in an architect-designed house. Its owners are proud of it in a different way from most house-proud people. You might notice it the minute you walk in. If the owners are the kind of people who welcome you to their house with a cup of coffee, you enter naturally into the kitchen area directly from the entrance without going through a formal living room. The architect arranged the spaces that way to suit their living style.

Or you might have noticed that you'd been in the house for hours and had no idea where the bedrooms were. No accident there — houses should have private spaces separated from public spaces mentally as well as physically.

It might have been something so obvious as a built-in seating arrangement near a fireplace that seemed to grow out of a wall, or a stunning and unexpected view through a wall of glass that seemed a part of, not separate from, nature, or changes of level to differentiate areas instead of walls and doors. Or it could have been something more subtle, such as a dark ceramic tile floor set off by pure white walls, or built-in concealed lighting which made lamps unnecessary.

Whatever it was, the owners didn't have to tell you that their house wasn't like the one next to it. Nor did they tell you it had been designed for them. The house told you that, and much about them as well. Architect-designed houses are like that.

They are often more than that, however. There is usually a timeless quality about them which did not easily reveal itself when they were built. Their owners do not feel the need to 'trade up' after a few years of living in them, because the houses are so much extensions of their own personalities that leaving would be painful, and more importantly, the house was and always would be adequate to their needs.

Traditional wisdom says that architect-designed houses are more costly than typical developer-built homes. As usual, there is a good reason for this bit of folk wisdom. For decades now, the clients of architects have been, for the most part, quite affluent, and naturally, the houses designed for them have reflected that affluence. But times have changed. Our entire society has become affluent, and, as far as housing is concerned, this has meant tremendous increases in the average cost of houses: from $30,000 in the fifties and $40,000 in the sixties, to now, in the late seventies, when the *average* cost of a new developer-built house has risen to well over $60,000.

And what of architect-designed houses? There are no national average costs available for custom-designed houses. But the houses featured in this book had per-square-foot costs when built which compared very favorably to average per-square-foot costs of developer-built houses during those periods.

It is not the premise of this book that architect-designed houses cost the same or less than developer-built houses. What the houses in this book should prove is that architects can (and do) design affordable houses — houses which offer their owners much, much more value for their housing dollars than would typically be obtained in developer-built houses.

The houses in this book have all appeared in the pages of *Architectural Record*, many of them in the Record Houses issues which each year present a selection of houses which, in the opinions of the editors of *Architectural Record*, represent the best examples of good design among the entries. The point is that while their inclusion in this book is the result of their good design at reasonable cost, they were originally published principally for reasons of design, although other considerations were taken into account.

In regard to specific prices, we have updated published costs (where they appeared) via a note at the bottom of the page giving an estimated 1978 cost of construction. This estimate was achieved by the use of data obtained from the Federal Home Loan Bank Board. We converted to percentage cost increases in the average prices of new houses for each year since 1966, and the appropriate percentage was used to multiply the published cost and arrive at the estimated 1978 cost.

There is, of course, no guarantee that any of these houses could be constructed today for that amount. Land costs are not included in these prices, nor is the cost of financing considered. According to informed opinion in the housing industry, it is these costs (land and financing) which are increasing most rapidly.

But building these same houses again is not — definitely not — the goal of this book. It is the house designed for *you* that is our concern. So turn the pages, and decide for yourself if the custom-designed house you've been dreaming about isn't really an *affordable* dream. If you agree, then now's the time to start looking for land, hire an architect, build your dream house, and as my friend, the distinguished Editor of *Architectural Record*, Walter F. Wagner, Jr., says, live happily ever after.

Chapter One:

INGENIOUS SOLUTIONS

Introduction

Designing houses for limited budgets is not easy. In addition to all the problems inherent in designing for an individual client, the architect is often faced with a site which is less than optimal, or the need for the use of inexpensive materials or labor-saving construction techniques. To achieve these ends and still come up with an attractive house design is the essence of the classic architectural dilemma. Each of the houses in this chapter represents a different solution to the problem, each equally valid and each totally unique.

What should you be looking for in these houses? First, look at the site and see how the architect has taken advantage of its opportunities or responded to its problems. Architect Dwight Holmes (p. 4) uses solid walls to screen off possibly unwelcome future development, while architects Cannady (p. 6) and McKim (p. 2) use other methods to widen narrow lots, and Richard Abbott (Traverso house, p. 16) uses yet another. The Riley house, set among evergreens and rocks (p. 12) and the Schafer house, ten feet from a running stream (p. 8), show how sites with more to offer can be well utilized by differing responses to similar opportunities.

Next, see what techniques were used to keep the project within the budget. The houses featured in this chapter range from plain concrete-block walls indoors and out (Holmes) to post-and-beam construction (McKim); from keeping square footage down (Riley) to simple and straightforward detailing (Cannady).

Finally, judge for yourself the excellence of the architect's response to the total problem by determining whether the house fits its site, suits its owners, and most importantly, stands, apart from considerations of budget, as an example of good design. Ultimately, these houses (and yours!) will be judged for their quality of design by people who know nothing of how much they cost.

The trick, after all, is not to build an inexpensive house — anyone can do that — but to build all the house you want on a budget you can afford.

John Oldenkamp photos

BR.

OPEN

BR.

BR.

OPEN

N

UPPER LEVEL   5

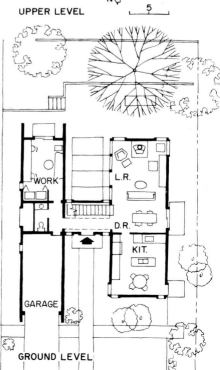

WORK

L.R.

D.R.

KIT.

GARAGE

GROUND LEVEL

AN H-SHAPED PLAN CREATES PRIVATE COURTYARDS

Economy and privacy were two important design criteria for architect Paul McKim's own townhouse. Built on a small, narrow lot, flanked on both sides by neighboring houses, the residence affords the McKims a good deal of privacy, and a nice sense of the outdoors.

For a house containing 1,600 square feet of living space, the construction cost was extremely low, especially when the beautifully detailed results are considered. Costs were kept to the budget by using a wood-frame, post-and-beam construction with large plaster panels on both the interior and exterior surfaces.

Basically, the design consists of two rectangular wings linked by a stairwell (see plan at left). The two courtyards, formed between the wings, give the desired outdoor space and privacy.

The house is zoned so that the children use the left wing and the parents the right. This means of zoning seems to be a good answer to maintaining a level of privacy suitable to

both parents and children. The children's bedrooms were placed over the "work" area, which could double as a play room in bad weather.

The interior is enlivened by opening up of the one-story space in the dining area to two-story spaces on both sides—in the living room, and in part of the kitchen.

An especially nice attention to details is evident in this house. Everything—from the trellis which spans the front courtyard and casts strong shadows down the white plaster wall (see photo right), to the hooded balcony over the garage—achieves the greatest effect by the simplest means. Even the white walls of the courtyard serve the secondary purpose of reflecting the sun into the north side of the living room.

Architect and owner: Paul W. McKim. *Location:* San Diego, Calif. *Landscape architect:* Wimmer & Yamada. *Interior designer:* Dixon Morrow Jr. *Contractor:* John Worobec.

1978: $43,260

2

Despite such a small budget, he has achieved striking spaces—including the big two-story living room and a variety of outdoor areas as well.

Wade Swicord photos

The Holmes House

Architect Dwight Holmes' house on Tampa Bay seems very much at home in what he calls "a near perfect example of semi-tropical environment: moderate temperatures, bright sun, generous rainfall and daily breezes off the Bay and Gulf." Placed well back from the street on a long and narrow lot, the house looks east across the open bay. Largely solid side walls of unfinished concrete block screen the house from uncertain future development on adjoining properties. The end elevations, however, are completely transparent. Four-panel sliding aluminum window walls stacked three high (left) form those façades. To control sun and to provide protection from tropical storms, a system of adjustable redwood louvers has been provided. The louvers have a shadow texture whose scale is adequately proportioned to the masonry planes. Within the severe rectangular volume, Holmes has created an appropriate openness by placing the dining and master bedroom platforms on the second and third floors at opposite ends of the plan, permitting two-story spaces for both living and dining rooms. The central utility core is designed to minimize interruptions of ventilation flow. Including central air conditioning for periods of intense heat and humidity, the house and a small studio behind it of similar construction cost $28,000.

Architect and owner: Dwight E. Holmes. *Location:* Tampa, Florida. *Contractor:* Ranon and Jimenez.

THIRD FLOOR

1978: $47,320

SECOND FLOOR

FIRST FLOOR

4

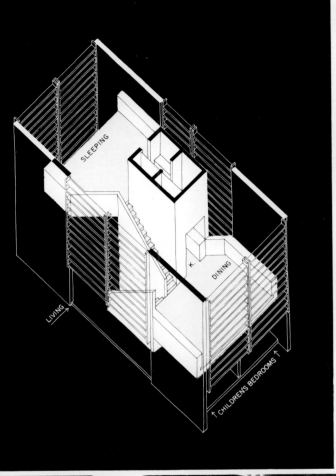

Alternating platforms above the ground floor (section left) create two-story spaces in the living room (below) and the dining room (above) The interior kitchen, open at both ends (right), is well-ventilated and has a good view of activities in the living room as well as outside on the terrace and the adjacent beach.

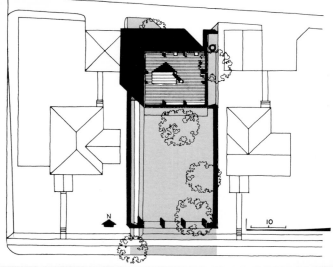

Jonathan King

In designing a house for his own family of four, in a Houston subdivision, architect William Cannady began with two important design decisions. First, he set the house at the rear of the lot creating in this way one large outdoor area instead of two smaller areas and avoiding the standard shoulder-to-shoulder relationship with neighbors. Second, he placed the house over the garage and developed an inviting roof terrace that provided a second usable outdoor space—this one to be used primarily by parents for cocktails and cookouts. The six-foot side yard restrictions and the pattern of existing trees combined to determine the precise siting as well as the 33- by 37-foot outside dimensions.

Kitchen, study, dining and living room, share the second floor and flow easily around a sharply defined central core. The level above is compartmentalized into parents' and children's bedrooms and baths. The floor of the master bedroom is cut back to create a narrow vertical connection with living room below (section and photo, opposite page).

The structure is standard wood frame, clad inside and out with 1-by 6-inch rough sawn cedar siding. Painted sheetrock is used selectively on ceilings and third floor partitions. The floor of the living room level is finished in clay tile imported from Mexico and the roof terrace is 1- by 4-inch redwood decking constructed in pallets.

The budget for this simply constructed but appealing house was $48,000, or just under $15 per square foot. According to Cannady, this very low cost was achieved for several reasons. The quantity and cost of finish materials was not excessive. But beyond that, almost no unusual detailing conditions were allowed to creep into the drawings and the contractor understood, and was sympathetic to, the architect/owners's rather straightforward design intention from the outset.

Architect and *owner:* WILLIAM T. CANNADY. *Location:* Houston, Texas. *Engineers:* Krahl & Gaddy (structural). *Landscape architect:* Carlisle Becker. *Contractor:* Design Fabricators, Gene Hopkins, partner-in-charge.

The creation of a rooftop terrace brought the useable outdoor coverage to virtually 100 per cent of the site—an objective that seems especially sensible for a small lot in a warm climate. Projecting vents are carefully located to intrude as little as possible (photo left). A solid parapet and surrounding trees help to preserve a pleasant sense of privacy when the roof deck is in use.

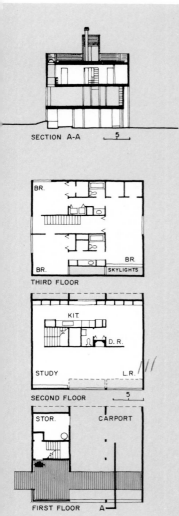

SECTION A-A   5

BR.

BR.   BR.
          SKYLIGHTS
THIRD FLOOR

KIT
          D.R.
STUDY   L.R.
SECOND FLOOR   5

STOR.   CARPORT

FIRST FLOOR   A

Photos by Richard Payne except as noted

1978: $81,600

Otto Baitz photos

CUT-OUTS FROM A CUBE CREATE A STRIKING FORM

Home-made houses have an important place in American tradition. But few ever claim to be architecture. However this 30-foot cube, set gently into nature not far from Woodstock, seems to combine the wholesome ingenuousness of the *Whole Earth Catalogue* with the formal purity of Ledoux's visionary projects of the 18th century.

The powerful geometry of the cube, unexpected in a rural place, overrides simple construction techniques—plywood on a steel and wood frame—and the resultant effect is one of freedom within order, old living happily with new. For instance, the crusty small-paned window panels, right, were taken from a nearby greenhouse about to be destroyed and incorporated into the house as it was being built.

All of this could seem quite contrived if it did not so accurately represent the lifestyle of the owners. The chaplain of Bard College and his wife, a serious pianist, are two mature and highly sophisticated people. They needed a house that would not impose a regime on them but rather would easily accept their existing pattern of living. But neither would their budget allow for one of those spacious houses that have a specially-designed room for everything.

The product of that program was built largely by the family with their son, Paul Shafer, in charge. It stands just ten feet from a rushing stream. In the spring flood waters come under the house but other times the brook seems to go out of its way to skirt the building. The 45-degree glazed corners enable a person standing next to the center-post of the house on the mezzanine to look out of the dining room window and see the stream approaching, then turn clockwise to watch it pass the tall living room window. Finally, turning another 90 degrees, he sees it disappear over the falls just below the house.

Architects: James B. Baker of Baker and Blake. *Associate architect:* Alex Wade. *Owners:* Rev. and Mrs. Frederick Q. Shafer. *Location:* Annandale-on-Hudson, New York. *Structural engineer:* Robert Silman. *Mechanical engineers:* Flack and Kurtz. *Contractor (foundations and steel erection):* Dittmar and Regg.

Each floor of the three-story house has a distinctly different quality. The spacious living room, lowest floor, has two low areas, the conservatory and fireplace corners, joined by a two-story space. The kitchen and dining room seem small in comparison but share both the tall space and the light which pours in from every side. The top floor, divided into many small rooms, provides a private place for each person.

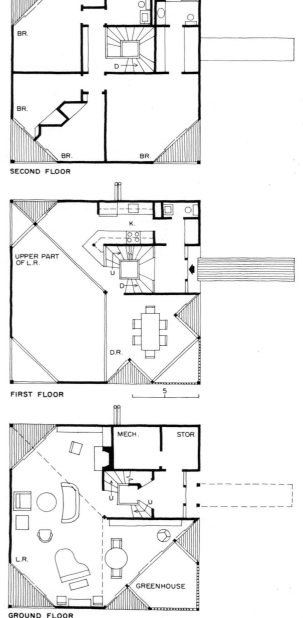

1978: $60,900

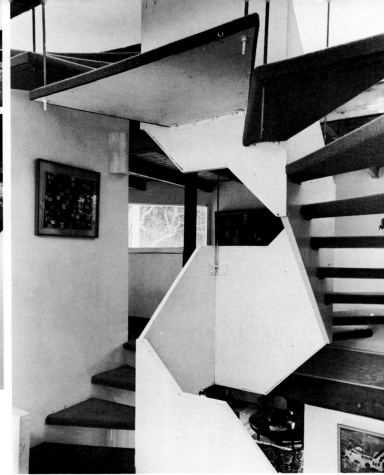

The two primary functions of the house, openness to nature and service of highly-developed lifestyles, are apparent on the interior. As one approaches the entrance, above left, on the bridge, the transparency of the house is conveyed by the multi-faceted glazing of the conservatory and above it, the dining room. From the entry, one goes down half-a-flight on the suspended plywood stair, top, to the living room or up to the dining room. The slender post in the middle of the house, above, is four steel angles. The furniture and objets d'art of the house, opposite, highly personal but displayed with assuredness, convey the diversity of the life lived here.

Philip Molten photos

A SMALL BUT CAREFULLY DETAILED WOODLAND HOUSE

Within the simplest imaginable structural framework of this small (under 1,000 square feet) house, architect J. Alexander Riley has created an extraordinary variety of indoor and outdoor spaces. Essentially, as is best seen in the plan and photo at right, the house is made of two flatroofed units set seven feet apart and bridged by a handsomely framed pitched roof set above twin clerestories that pour light into the center of the house, even though it is on a northeastern slope.

That roof is one of four elements that give distinction and interest to what—in less sensitive hands—could have been quite ordinary. The second design device was staggering the ends of the elements—on both the entry and view ends of the plan—to eliminate any sense of boxiness. Third: dropping the living room floor three steps, and leaving it open to the dining room and kitchen to add a sense of spaciousness. Finally, while the house is of the simplest construction, with posts, single-thickness walls of 2¼- by 6-inch cedar and a single-thickness 2 by 6 cedar roof—great attention was paid to the detailing. Note for example the mitered corners of the clerestory structure (photo right) and the simple-to-fabricate but effective detailing of the interior (photos next page).

Architect and *owner:* J. Alexander Riley. *Location:* Inverness, California. *Contractor:* Jean Madill Burroughs.

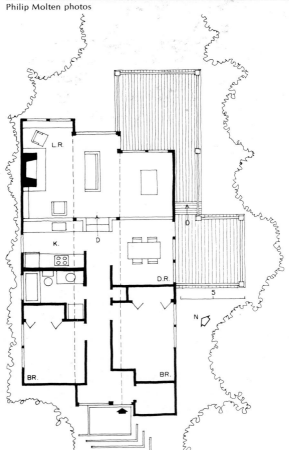

On the interiors, the simple wood framing is clearly expressed, with a small but effective amount of trim and special detailing. The photo (far right) shows the main view wall, with the deck beyond. At right, a view from the living room to the dining room and kitchen three steps above. The kitchen-living room, photo below, emphasizes the changes in scale and room shape worked out within, again, an essentially simple framework.

This warm, comfortable three-level house, with a structure formed by a series of tall Y-shaped "trees," was designed on a moderate budget for a young Colorado family. The owners wanted a house that would affirm its natural mountain setting. Aside from their obvious connotation, the architect felt that the "trees" relate to the forms of many mining structures still seen in the mountains west of Denver.

Made by sandwiching 2 x 6s, 2 x 10s, and 2 x 12s, the "trees" were fabricated on the ground, then hoisted into position. Because the house is anchored to the ground only by the trees, site grading and foundation work were kept to a minimum. The exterior balconies, which are suspended from the structure by cables, seem to float over the site.

The living, dining and library areas are continuous on the entrance level to provide an open space for the full 42-foot width of the house. The balcony-bridge connects the stair with the parents' bedroom and dressing area, bath, utility, and guest rooms. On the below-grade level, open on one side because of the ground slope, are two children's bedrooms closed off by folding doors. Opened, the doors provide another 42-foot area to be used for play on stormy days.

Windows, placed high on the facade, let light into the house while keeping the interior private from the street (see photo below).

The exterior materials are rough-sawn cedar siding, with fir posts and beams. Cedar is used again in the interior along with white plaster board for the walls, and quarry tile for the floors.

Architects: Ream, Quinn & Associates—projectdesign: James T. Ream, 1761 Green Street, San Francisco. Owners: Mr. and Mrs. Peter Lipman; associate architects: David L. Van Wormer and Childress; structural engineers: Ketchum, Konkel, Ryan & Hastings; contractor: Burton A. Payne.

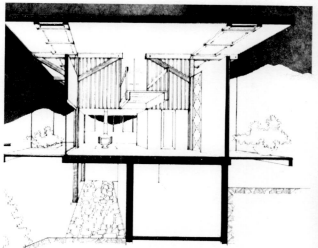

Set on a steep hillside facing the Rocky Mountains, this house achieves the sense of sheltered warmth desired by its young owners without sacrificing any of the view. Standing outside on the balcony (see photo left), which is hung from a system of structural "trees" by steel cables, would be an invigorating experience at any time. On the inside, two large open areas give a feeling of spaciousness.

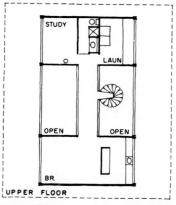

STUDY

LAUN

OPEN   OPEN

BR.

UPPER FLOOR

MUSIC

L.R.

DINING   K.

MAIN FLOOR

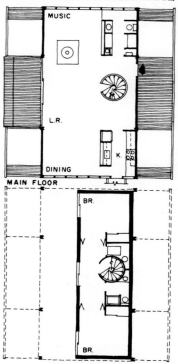

BR.

BR.

LOWER FLOOR   5

1978: $74,160

Roger Ewy photos

Panel walls are hung free from the poles by brackets, so the structure "reads" from the outside. The glazing, shown in the detail below, is fixed for added savings; ventilation comes instead from louvers in the panels. Interior lighting increases the great drama of the house at night.

FIRST FLOOR   5   MEZZANINE FLOOR

D.R.
K.
L.R.
BR.

BR.
STUDIO

1"x4" T&G
VERTICAL SIDING

WOOD COL.
GLASS

A SOPHISTICATED POLE HOUSE FOR THE SUBURBS

Economy and a great sense of space have been achieved for this sophisticated little weekend house by its ingenious structure composed of a system of 20-foot-high wood poles.

The house was designed for a single client who came to the architect with a small budget and a 60-foot-wide suburban lot. This had houses on three sides and no interesting site features except one large tree. The architect's idea was to make up in the interior space what was lacking in the site: the interior volume was to be a site itself.

A seven-foot-high fence and wooden curtain walls were strategically placed to block off neighbors, and visually preserve a sense of airiness and light. The poles support the space, but do not break it up.

Placed on a grid of room-sized 10-foot bays, these poles carry roof, balcony and panel loads, and create a marvelously expansive flow of space which admirably fulfills the architect's intent—but keeps within the client's budget.

Privacy is assured inside, and space usage defined, by changes in level which add to the drama of the structural frame. A living "room" is two steps down; the owner's bedroom, guest room and study are tucked in mezzanines bolted to the poles. "The different elevations," comments the architect, give "controlled views of the foliage and sky—up and out" as well as secluded lookouts on the inside space below.

The design strength of the little house derives as much from the expression of these natural wood materials, which are left exposed, as from the dynamic organization of the single space and the strong, contrasting geometry of the structural frame.

Architect: Richard Owen Abbott. *Owner:* Miss Joan Traverso. *Location:* Westbrook, Connecticut. *Interior design:* Richard O. Abbott. *Contractor:* George C. Field Co.

1978: $35,150

A study-balcony, right, shelters the entry and extends through the outside wall as a deck for added open space. The sunken sitting area focuses on the red-painted stove-pipe chimney. Sparing use of primary colors adds spatial depth throughout.

Norman McGrath photos

This crisp multi-leveled house, relating closely to the slope and character of this small, heavily wooded plot, was designed on a minimum budget by architect Jerry Weisbach. Since the owners wished to preserve the nature of the site while achieving a sense of spaciousness around and within the house, the architect split the house into two rectangular wings and placed them on different ground levels. Consequently, the house is viewed upon approach as a series of broad parallel planes, each of which recedes and descends a bit further into the woods. The result appears quite large, and yet an integral part of the site.

Each of the elements performs a distinct function (see plan below), with the wing nearest the street—containing two bedrooms above the garage—connected to the living wing by a stair tower (shaded in section and plan). The separation of living and sleeping areas into two wings gives the family a great deal of privacy. Privacy was also the factor in shielding the outside balcony off the master bedroom from the street by extending the front wall across it (photo, top right). All other living areas are related directly to the outdoors by large expanses of glass.

A change in ceiling heights throughout the house provides a variety of spatial experiences, variety which is carried into the two-story living room by placing a studio-den on an interior balcony. The interior has been kept in the spirit of the exterior by treating all wall surfaces as simple planes.

The beautifully detailed exterior, clad in redwood siding, reflects the natural surroundings. Left untreated, the redwood will weather with time.

Architect: **Gerald G. Weisbach** of Weisbach/Boutmy/Silver, 55 Stevenson Street San Francisco, California. Owners: *Mr. and Mrs. Medford Schwarz*; engineer: *Fong Chan*; contractor: *A. Von Rotz.*

1978: $63,233

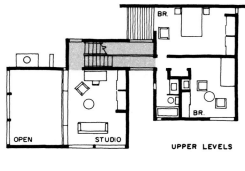

UPPER LEVELS

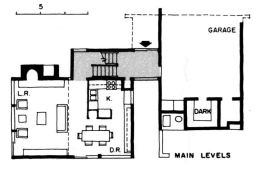

MAIN LEVELS

Built essentially as a series of intersecting planes, this house for a heavily wooded site affords a great deal of privacy for its owners. The various interior levels are designed to closely follow the slope of the site. Extremely controlled detailing gives the design a sense of crispness.

Karel Bauer photos

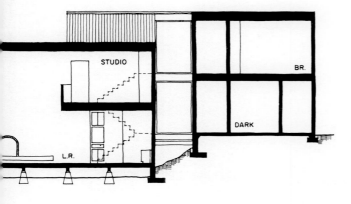

STUDIO

BR.

DARK

L.R.

"That's technology for you—prestressed adobe!"

Chapter Two:

HEIRS TO THE INDUSTRIAL REVOLUTION

Introduction

What follows is not a fable. Early English houses were built of post-and-beam construction, with posts often set five to eight feet apart, and the intervening spaces filled with stone and mortar. Fireplaces were built of brick and mortar, however, with bricks eight inches long and four inches wide (for coursing). To fit into these fireplaces, firewood was cut two bricks in length, or sixteen inches long. When lath-and-plaster construction began to appear, laths were split from firewood and thus had to be nailed to studs set sixteen inches apart. We *still* build houses with studs on sixteen-inch centers 400 years later. So much for progress in housing construction.

The houses in this chapter are, in at least one aspect or another, somewhat closer to modern industrial technology. The Bohlin house (p. 28), with its factory windows and industrial light at the entrance, is a happy example of technology at home in the woods. The corrugated metal-clad exterior walls of the Bruder house (p. 24) holds four-inch batts of insulation in response to hot desert days and cold desert nights. In the Brandzel house (p. 34), the architects have made what is most often hidden, a roof-supporting truss, into the dominant visual characteristic.

Other houses in this chapter show the use of prefabricated components such as chimneys and fireplaces and stressed-skin walls. Where reactionary building codes do not prevent them from doing so and clients are knowledgeable enough to sense the advantages and aesthetic values of components whose beauty is inherent in their functions, architects can often utilize the best that modern technology has to offer.

The point of the non-fable which began this chapter, and the point to look for in the houses which follow, is that technology can be beautiful — if we let it. Unfortunately, architects sometimes tend to feel diffident about using these materials and techniques in houses for clients because some clients don't appreciate them, even though architects often use them in their own houses. If (like me) you do appreciate them, (and I hope you do), be sure to let your architect know about it. He might have some really neat ideas for your house!

Photos: James Brett

The client, Joseph P. Burke, hoping to build a weekend house on a low budget, had investigated builder and prefab houses before he engaged Rotner. Through strict economy of space and materials, the architect was able to keep the costs down to approximately $21 per square foot (1970-71) for a total of $34,000.

The house on a one-half-acre site in Watermill, Long Island overlooks a lake. Because of the high water table, only the garage is at grade. The utility room and first floor bedroom and bath are five steps up, the living room, terrace and kitchen are at midpoint and high enough for a view, and two additional bedrooms are at the top level, one of which overlooks the kitchen and serves as a study.

The three masonry walls of the garage carry most of the house. The floor joists of the kitchen and living room are laid on the two parallel bearing walls of the garage and the bedrooms are stacked vertically. As the section indicates, the kitchen and living rooms share a

12-foot ceiling. A secondary wall on the lake side (overleaf) serves as a *bris soleil* and frames the views. The principal entrance is inset and reached by a flight of stairs (opposite page, right). The window above lights the stairway and entrance hall.

Economies include a prefab chimney and fireplace, stock windows, conventional framing sheathed on the exterior and interior with one layer of grooved plywood and simple metal post and cable railings. Since the decks project over open space they didn't require flashing or waterproofing. Built-ins were done by carpenters on the site, rather than by cabinet shops. The single expensive item in the construction was the use of insulated glass throughout.

The Burke house was designed primarily for a bachelor. The two additional sleeping areas on the top level and the additional bath assures that it can go on the market as a family house.

Robert L. Rotner

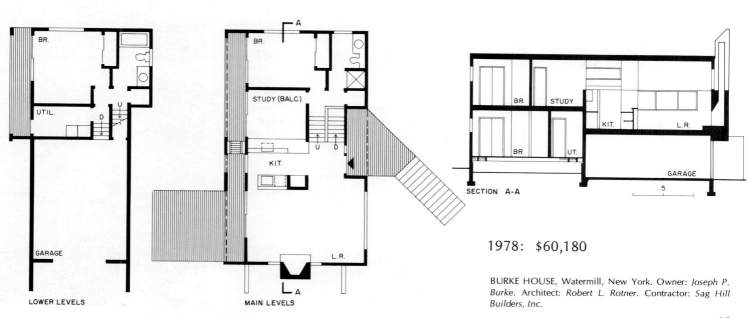

LOWER LEVELS

MAIN LEVELS

SECTION A-A

1978: $60,180

BURKE HOUSE, Watermill, New York. Owner: *Joseph P. Burke*. Architect: *Robert L. Rotner*. Contractor: *Sag Hill Builders, Inc.*

Bruder residence
New River, Arizona
William Bruder, Architect

This modest house, carefully sited in a relatively empty stretch of desert north of Phoenix, was designed by its owner and constructed with the help of friends in just over a month, using the simplest kinds of materials and details. A good deal of forethought and invention went into its planning, however. The result is an unusually expressive small house and studio that are fine-tuned to the climate and constructed for under $13,000—or roughly eleven dollars per square foot.

The house is conventionally framed in wood stud with 2 x 10 floor joists supporting a fiberboard subfloor. The roof structure is composed of 3 x 8 fir beams on four-foot centers. Insulation is applied throughout: four-inch batts in the stud walls and a two-inch thickness of rigid urethane under the red roll roofing. The exterior, though, is unexpectedly clad in galvanized metal sheet. Because it is corrugated and matte finished, it does not throw off eye-searing reflections under the bright sun. Instead, it produces softly-glowing reflections of the surrounding desert—reflections that change perceptibly as the days and seasons pass.

To the right in the plan (above) is a small drafting studio with two work spaces. Opposite the studio, across the entry breezeway, is the main living space, which also doubles for dining and sleeping. It backs against a kitchen, bath and dressing area. Nearly every space is detailed for multiple use.

Unifying the two halves of the structure is a generously-scaled, trellised deck that faces a deep arroyo and undisturbed natural desert beyond. Here is the outdoor center of activity, a space for a wide variety of uses day or night. This north exposure is completely glazed while the openings on the other three elevations are sharply controlled against the sun.

Space conditioning is achieved by an evaporative cooling unit with exposed ducts and a fireplace augmented by portable heaters for winter evenings.

Architect and owners:
Mr. & Mrs. William P. Bruder
Black Canyon Stage
New River, Arizona
Photographer: Neil Koppes

1978: $15,080

The shallow pitch of the roof is echoed in the tapered plan shapes which open to the north. The large glazed opening is shielded from the sun by an overhead trellis that casts elaborate shadow patterns across the deck and side walls.

UPPER FLOOR

MAIN FLOOR

The tall living room gives the house a spaciousness that is surprising given its size. Built-in furniture, interconnected spaces, and large windows looking into the woods in three directions also help expand the space. The section reveals a tiny, secluded roof deck reached by a ladder.

The Gueron House

In 1971, architect Henri Gueron built himself this three-bedroom house (including equipment, insulated, and finished interiors, as well as site work) for $15,000.

Gueron lists four ways by which he accomplished this feat: 1. Square footage was kept as low as possible, barely more than the zoning minimum of 975 square feet; 2. The house was designed on a 4- by 8-foot module, horizontally and vertically, since standard-size plywood was the ideal material for his design—both economically and esthetically; 3. Almost all prefabricated elements are also standard (the principal exception is the acrylic dome in the dining area which cost $110); 4. He served as his own general contractor for an estimated saving of 20 per cent and detailed the house to be easy to build. He estimates that done for a client using standard contract procedures, the cost would have been about $25,000.

The crisp exterior is ⅜-in. resin-impregnated plywood applied to the studs. The caulking is a white elastomeric sealant. Two coats of latex acrylic semi-gloss paint were used both on the exterior and on the drywall interiors. Finally, the bright accent colors of epoxy enamel were added. Placed diagonally on a long narrow lot studded with the scrub oak typical of eastern Long Island, the house is invisible from the road in summer but during the gray winter provides a brilliant flash of color for passers-by.

Architect and *owner:* Henri Gueron of Gueron and Lepp. *Location:* East Hampton, New York. *Engineer:* Ken Smith (electrical).

Ben Schnall photos

26

1978: $42,250

SECTION A-A

Its cedar siding stained green to blend with the leaves of a surrounding forest, this house—designed by architect Peter Bohlin for his parents—is in fine sympathy with a natural site of 18 acres in Cornwall, Connecticut. Seemingly modest from the approach (photo overleaf, top), the building is actually a carefully studied progression of vertically expanding spaces, which lead the visitor from the dark shade of evergreen trees at the drive and entry bridge into the high living room with a view of dappled sunlight through lacy deciduous branches.

An industrial-type light standard on the parking-lot side of the bridge begins a series of vertical, rust-red-painted orientation points in the visitor's progress. Others are the surrounds of the glazed front door, those round exposed-concrete columns that extend through the interior and—finally—the industrial-type framing of the living room windows expose the climactic view. The route over the bridge leads past the end of the building, which is only 12 feet wide, under the low roof of the porch, and down several flights of stairs until the full height of the living room is reached.

Careful attention to detail has made a dramatic product of simple materials such as corrugated aluminum for roofing, tongue-and-groove siding and circular concrete piers. Bohlin states that the contrast between large sheets of glass in the standard, black-finished sliding doors and the small panes of glass elsewhere (also standard) is intentional.

Costs for the 1,800-square-foot structure were just over $30 per foot. The project has won two awards for design.

- -

Architects: Bohlin and Powell
  partner-in-charge:
  Peter Bohlin
  project architect:
  Russell Roberts
  182 North Franklin Street
  Wilkes-Barre, Pennsylvania and
  Gateway Towers, Suite 235
  Pittsburgh, Pennsylvania
Owners: Mr. and Mrs. Eric Bohlin
Location: West Cornwall, Connecticut
Engineers: Rist-Frost Associates
Contractor: Olsen Brothers
Photographer: Joseph Molitor

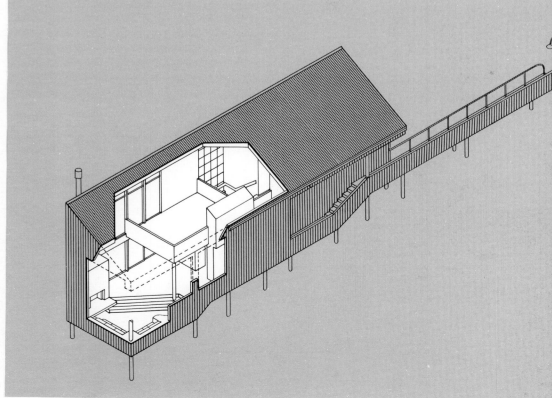

1978: $39/sq. ft.

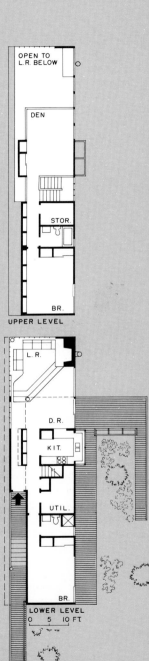

OPEN TO
L.R. BELOW

DEN

STOR.

BR.

UPPER LEVEL

L.R.

D.R.

KIT.

UTIL.

BR.

LOWER LEVEL
0   5   10 FT.

Seen from the entry side, the long shape is a transition from dark evergreen to sunlit forest (photo opposite, top). The view toward the kitchen (opposite, bottom) reveals the partial enclosure of the kitchen in a greenhouse-like structure. The stairs to the upper level (below, left) lead to the intimately scaled den (below, right) with its balcony-overlook of the living room.

The light gray finish of both walls and stained-oak flooring forms a soft-but-defined contrast to the darker colors of siding and structure.

A simply-constructed wood barrel vault transforms this straightforward post-and-beam vacation house into an elegant residence. Perched above a rambling creek near Wausa, Nebraska, the $20,000 building by architect Neil Astle makes use of folding doors to provide a maximum of five sleeping rooms. Triple 2 by 12 Western red cedar beams running the long dimension of the house as floor structure, both ways as roof structure, and supported by columns made up of two 2 by 10s and a 2 by 8 spacer, form the basic grid. Two-by-six decking is used on both roof and walls to enclose it.

The four semi-circular trusses which form the 15-foot diameter barrel vault (left) also use 2 by 12s. The paired curved sections cut from them have a two layer inner core of ¾-inch fir plywood all of which is glued (with exterior glue) and nailed together. All joints are carefully staggered; the semi-circular elements are braced by a double 2 by 12 bottom chord and a kingpost of 2 by 4s either side of a center 2 by 2 that interlocks top and bottom. Four-ply built-up roofing is used everywhere topped with gravel on the flat portion and roll roofing on the vault. A similar arched pergola of spaced 4 by 4s over the deck is planned for the future to deal with glare from the sky.

Architect: NEIL ASTLE of Neil Astle and Associates. *Owner:* Dr. and Mrs. R. L. Tollefson. *Location:* Wausa, Nebraska. *Engineer:* Robert Sullivan (mechanical). *Carpentry contractor:* Arnold Prather.

1978: $33,800

For a lakefront site that few readers will identify as Fremont, Nebraska, architects Bahr Hanna Vermeer & Haecker designed an unusual summer house using cedar recycled from an old sheep barn for decking and for all horizontal structural members.

To assure privacy from the street and from neighbors, the house has minimal window openings on three sides. All large glazed areas face the deck and the lake beyond. The dominant visual element on the lake side of the house is a deep, wood truss, used to stiffen the entire frame and to give spatial definition to important outdoor spaces—an open deck and screened porch.

The arrangement of indoor living areas is linear across the width of the site with sleeping areas—including closet-top guest bunks—confined to the second floor. A split-level entry stair links the two levels. An outdoor stair, just off the master bedroom, connects upper and lower decks.

In spite of its comparatively uncomplicated plan, the Brandzel house masses strongly and differently on every elevation. Wood forms are used boldly in simple but expressive blocks and planes which are finished in cedar siding laid up in alternating diagonal patterns—patterns repeated on the interiors in floor and wall finishes.

Constructed at just under $20 per square foot, the Brandzel residence makes a virtue of bold forms with plain vanilla details, and misses no opportunity to insist that living here should be relaxed and informal.

Its rather bold forms are in contrast with neighboring houses, but the somewhat featureless site seemed to demand a strong solution—a solution the architects worked with skill and sensitivity to provide.

1978: $28/sq. ft.

Architects: Bahr Hanna Vermeer & Haecker Architects, Ltd.
535 Nebraska Savings Building Omaha, Nebraska
Owners: Mr. and Mrs. Thomas Brandzel
Location: Fremont, Nebraska
Engineers: Donald Thomsen (mechanical)
Contractor: Larsen & Jipp
Photographer: Gordon Peery

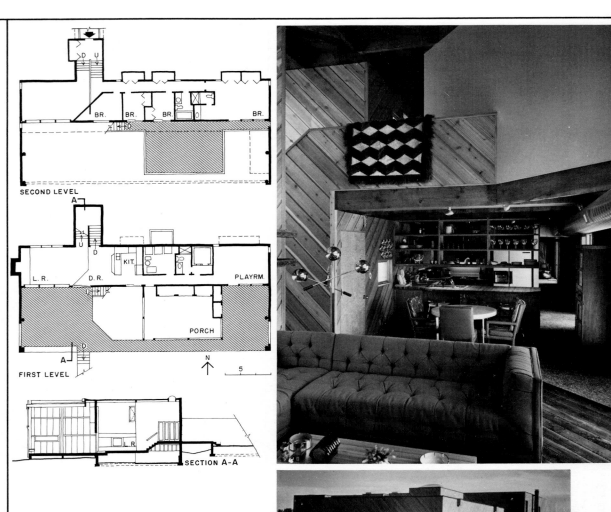

SECOND LEVEL

BR. BR. BR. BR.

FIRST LEVEL

L.R. D.R. KIT. PLAYRM. PORCH

N 5

SECTION A-A

L.R.

Plans and sections of the Brandzel residence show a strongly ordered concept but rather intricate volumes and massing. A consistent cloak of cedar siding unifies the massing.

L-D.

K.

FIRST FLOOR   5

BR.

BR.

SECOND FLOOR

A MINIMUM-COST HOUSE
TUCKED INTO A HILLSIDE

This rugged and very original little house grew out of an attempt to provide a specially-designed low-cost vacation home in a beautiful but remote area where building costs are high. It uses prefabricated stressed-skin panels for walls and floors, for an estimated 15 per cent saving over conventional wood frame. In addition to the Record Houses award winner, which was built for sale (right), two even lower-priced versions have been built, shown at left.

The patented structural panels consist of a plywood skin and a rigid, fire-resistant foam plastic core. The core insulates, and the plywood—redwood on the exterior and cedar or fir inside—also forms the finish.

The panels are four feet wide, and the real key to success came in using this module as the basis for efficient plans. The larger house has a 932-square-foot living area. It cost $15,000 in 1968, including a fully-equipped kitchen and bathroom, wall-to-wall indoor-outdoor carpets and electric floor and baseboard unit heating. The second, smaller house to the top left cost $12,000; the third, costing $10,000, was achieved with sleeping alcoves and the use of outdoor decks. Details for all three were designed to scuttle complicated on-site construction steps, and use simple joints and simple finishes from stock materials to help keep costs in line. The larger house took just three days to build, using a four-man crew.

Architect and *owner:* Sim Van der Ryn of Hirshen & Van der Ryn. *Location:* Point Reyes, California. *Contractor:* W. D. McAlvain.

Joshua Freiwald photos

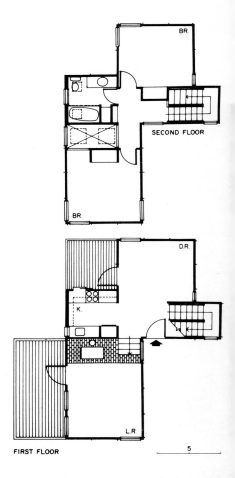

BR.

SECOND FLOOR

BR.

D.R.

K.

FIRST FLOOR   5

L.R.

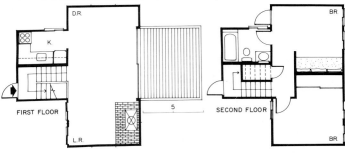

D.R.

K.

FIRST FLOOR

5

SECOND FLOOR

L.R.

BR.

BR.

1978: $27,750

A number of playful "extras" are built into the two-story, split-level design: The living room with its Franklin stove has a skylit, two-story "well." An over-look from the kitchen can be seen in the photos (below). Wherever possible, out-door decks are enlisted to increase living space without adding to foundation costs.

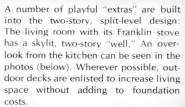

Chapter Three:

SNUG RETREATS

Introduction

Who hasn't dreamed of a little place, off in the woods, on a lake or at the beach, or up in the mountains, where we can, as they say, get away from it all? While log cabins, A-frames and precut chalets are okay, an architect-designed home away from home is nicer, no doubt about it.

It is important to note that the program (those goals the architect tries to meet) for a vacation house is different from the program for a house which will be lived in year round, though the four-season vacation house is included here. Typically, the vacation house will be smaller, more cozy, if you will, than the year-round house. It will relate to its setting in a more intimate manner. Amenities such as fireplaces and decks become more central to the conception. Informality is the keynote in the program, which will be obvious as you look at these houses. Minimum maintenance is a must, since who wants to spend vacations doing up-keep work?

Although a vacation house is generally meant for seasonal use, notice how attractive these houses would be in any season. That is, of course, one good criterion on which to base your judgment of these designs. A good design looks good all year round. Notice also that houses built for the mountains wouldn't look right at the shore. Site planning is as crucial for vacation houses as it is for permanent dwellings.

I have to admit that my favorite house of all the houses in this chapter is architect Wendell Lovett's little gem on Crane Island in Puget Sound (p. 44). There just isn't a wrong move made in this beautiful job. But that is very nearly true of every other house in this chapter, so it won't disturb me if you like another house better.

Joshua Freiwald photos

A house at Sea Ranch: informality expressed in plan, form and details

It used to be that "vacation house" meant a modest cottage in a lovely spot. While none of the houses in this collection are large or pretentious, Donald Sandy's house for Mr. and Mrs. John Crossman comes closest to that simple old-fashioned idea. The plan, the form and the details all express an informality that seems appropriate for rural living. However, informality does not mean shoddy or incomplete finish. For $23,000 architect Sandy has provided interiors, above right, with walls of the same diagonal resawn redwood boards as on the exterior, oak floors and a large fireplace of field stone found on the site. The massive chimney provides important shear resistance to the Pacific Ocean winds, which were carefully charted when Sea Ranch was conceived and which have contributed a groundhugging silhouette to this house and others built there. A future bedroom addition will supplement the sleeping loft which has a unique floor structure of laminated 2x4s.

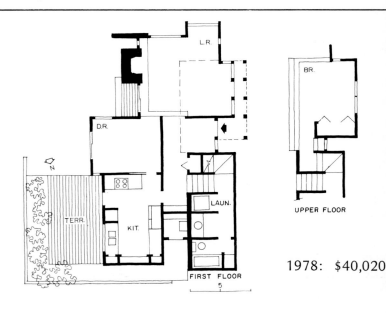

1978: $40,020

Location: Sea Ranch, Sonoma County, California. Owners: *Mr. and Mrs. John Crossman;* architect: *Donald Sandy, Jr.;* contractor: *Bill Pauley.*

The DeVido House

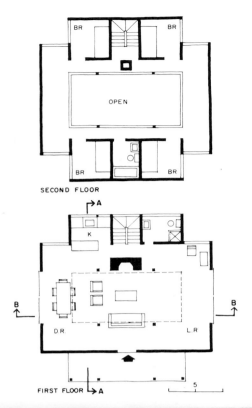

SECOND FLOOR

FIRST FLOOR

This sophisticated little vacation house epitomizes the reaction of city dwellers against the small, standardized rooms of today's apartments, and their strong desire for big, soaring spaces in their second homes in the country. As architect De Vido puts it, "I wanted a large living space—shaped, textured and dramatic—to contrast with the more mundane shapes of apartment living."

He has achieved this in a striking manner, and within an extremely reasonable budget—about $21,000 for the house alone in 1968. The heart of the concept is a big, three-story space, filled with sunlight. At the lower, living levels, this space extends to the outdoors through two sliding glass walls. Four bedrooms, small but adequate, and two fair-sized lounge/bunk areas are on the second or balcony level. At the very top are two aeries, reached by retractable ladders, for work and drafting. Big banks of windows on two sides provide light and views for these platform areas. These spaces, plus two baths and a small, open kitchen, provide most facilities of a very big house.

The house is situated on a long and narrow strip of woodland, and was designed to provide privacy on the two exposures closest to the neighboring lots and views of the woods and flowering shrubs on the other sides. The house is boldly symmetrical, with

1978: $38,850

the main approach on the center axis, via a covered entrance porch and a path from a parking area.

The design itself is a discerning, rustic understatement, with exposed structural parts and natural wood finishes used throughout. Variation and accent are achieved by texture—cedar shingle outside, rough-sawn cedar walls and polished white pine floors inside—and by a darker stain for the trim. The total effect is one of ease and warmth and freshness.

Architect and *owner:* Alfred De Vido.
Location: East Hampton, New York.
Contractor: Pete De Castro.

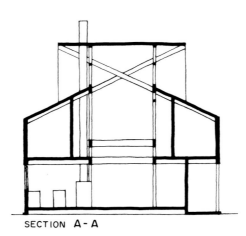

SECTION A-A

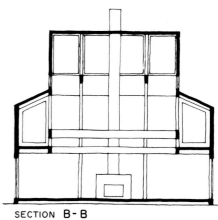

SECTION B-B

The structure consists of a basic Douglas fir post-and-girt system (on a 5-foot module), plus four central columns and "x" trusses to support the highest roof. The exterior wall is insulated, and all glass is insulating, to allow electric heat in winter.

© Ezra Stoller (ESTO) photos

Christian Stub photos

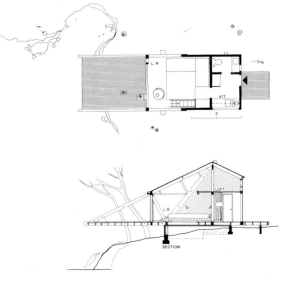

Christian Staub photos

The site: Crane Island in Puget Sound's San Juan Island Group. The architect and owner: Wendell Lovett. His program: a small, low-maintenance vacation retreat for his own family that would provide a holiday atmosphere and a complete change from urban routine.

The resulting structure is only 12 feet wide and contains just 370 square feet of enclosed space including a small sleeping loft reached from inside by a simple ladder-stair. Inverted bow-string trusses support the roof and suspend the deck that cantilevers 18 feet over the foundations. Within this structure, Lovett has fitted a compact kitchen, plumbing essentials, minimum storage and space for sitting and sleeping

six. All furniture is built-in. The level of the deck drops one step (the depth of the joists—see section) inside to accommodate the mattress seating.

Much of the fun of this house comes from the boldness of the concept: the tightness of the plan contrasted against the audacity of the long cantilever, as well as from the skill with which the house exploits the site and view. The detailing is neat and clean throughout but never fussy, and retains a very pleasant and appropriate sense of informality.

In form and color, the interiors carry through the design theme stated so simply and forcefully on the exteriors. There is no wasted motion in the design and hardly a

space or element that is not put to multiple use. Of all the houses in this collection, perhaps none is conceived and executed with more singleness of purpose or realizes its design goals more completely.

All structural lumber is Douglas fir. Exterior and interior cladding is rough sawn cedar stained to match the bark of surrounding trees. Cost of construction was approximately $15,000. A beautiful site; a challenging program; a neat and imaginative solution.

LOVETT VACATION HOUSE, Crane Island, Washington. Architect: *Wendell Lovett.* Structural engineer: *Robert Albrecht.* Contractor, *architect with Clifford I. Hooper.*

1978: $23.550

Architect: GIOVANNI PASANELLA
Owners: Mr. and Mrs. Charles Dunbar
Location: Winhall, Vermont
Associate: Etel Thea Kramer
Structural engineer: Stanley Gleit
Contractor: Cyril Hoyt, Jr.

Within this neat and fairly unassuming ski house is a truly spectacular space. All major living areas extend, balcony-like, off a three-story-high, glassed-in stair well to form an exceptionally dramatic and spacious interior.

The owners, Mr. and Mrs. Dunbar, have three married daughters, and wanted a house that would be comfortable for them alone, or for any combination of visiting children, grandchildren or friends. While the prime function of the house was to serve as a base for days of active skiing, the Dunbars wanted a lively and commodious interior for evenings and days of bad weather, and a design equally suitable for a summer vacation retreat.

The site is on a mountain slope, across a valley from Stratton Mountain and its ski facilities. A three-story scheme with varied angles of orientation was developed to give the best possible views across the countryside.

In developing the design, architect Pasanella says he wished "to create a house in which all rooms but bedrooms would share a volume of space, yet retain some physical and visual separation." He accomplished this by devising a plan of two diagonally inter-locking squares: a three-story void occurs at the triangular intersection, enclosed from the outside by a glass screen. Pasanella adds, "the living spaces revolve and climb about this open well, each borrowing the well's space, and making each room larger than its actual floor area. The two staircases climbing the well are made of the lightest possible steel elements to interfere minimally with the space." The resulting house is very comfortable, practical, and provides interesting spaces for activities of all age groups.

The approximate cost, excluding lot, landscaping and furnishings, was $31,000.

1978: $57,350

The basically wood-framed house is supported by exposed, round concrete columns which diminish in diameter by three inches at each floor level, forming ledges for the framing members. The exterior and the continuous space inside are sheathed in red cedar clapboards.

David Hirsch photos

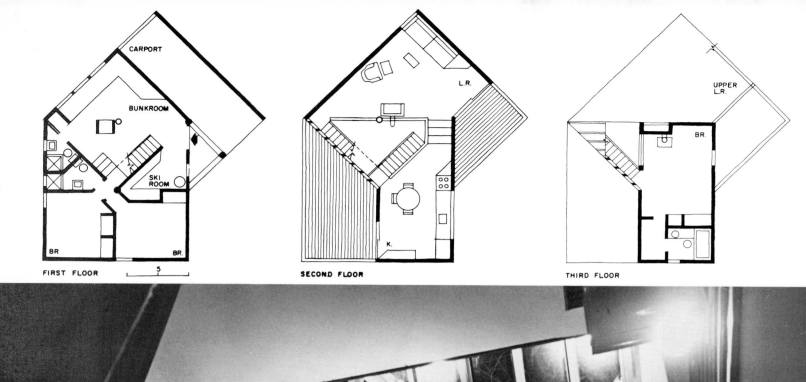

FIRST FLOOR |—— 5 ——|

SECOND FLOOR

THIRD FLOOR

On the lower level of the Dunbar house, a multi-purpose room serves as a sitting room or as bunkroom and playroom for children; three steps lower are two private bedrooms. The middle level includes a space for cooking and eating, and a living room and adjoining outdoor deck. On the highest level is the master bedroom.

On the interior, the clapboard sheathing does not meet at the corners, to leave the structural members exposed at corners, base and ceiling; the exposed framing is enameled white and forms rail tops, door frames and edges of built-in clapboard benches and cabinets. All ceilings are gypsum board and incorporate electric radiant-heating panels. Windows and skylights are insulating glass, except for a plastic dome skylight in the master dressing room, which doubles as a hatchway to the roof. Floors are slate in heavy-duty areas (entry, ski room, bunkroom, kitchen and baths); others are red fir, with red cedar for the decks.

Without power tools, without heavy equipment, without, in fact, outside help of any important kind, the Kindorf family, five-strong, built this appealing, three-level cabin on a two-acre site in Plumas County, California. The site is choked with pine and dips down to a large creek where swimming and trout fishing are seasonal preoccupations. The cabin was built over a period of three summers with cabinetwork and furniture construction occupying the long winter months in between.

The cabin has no electricity. Light is provided by kerosene lamps and heat by a Franklin stove. A 500-gallon, gravity-fed water tank supplies domestic needs and sewage wastes are chemically treated and stored. The absence of modern conveniences is in no way deprivative, for the family agrees that the simplified life style that results is fun and greatly heightens the sense of place.

Clad in cedar board and batten over plywood sheathing and 4- by 4-inch wood studs, the cabin has a simplicity and structural logic plainly visible in the photos. Its living and sleeping arrangements have a pleasant informality and its detailing and finishes are minimal.

Because of its inherent modesty and the very special circumstances surrounding its construction, the Kindorf cabin was built for the astonishingly low figure of $5 per square foot.

Architect and owner: Robert Kindorf
   245 Draeger Drive
   Moraga, California
Location: Plumas County, California
Contractors: The Kindorf family
Photographer: Philip Molten

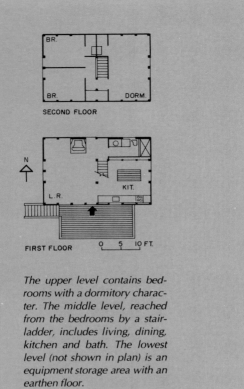

SECOND FLOOR

N

FIRST FLOOR 0 5 10 FT.

The upper level contains bedrooms with a dormitory character. The middle level, reached from the bedrooms by a stairladder, includes living, dining, kitchen and bath. The lowest level (not shown in plan) is an equipment storage area with an earthen floor.

1978: $7/sq. ft.

Phokion Karas photos.

UPPER FLOOR

LIVING   BR.

DINING   KIT.   BR.

5

LOWER FLOOR

GAME   UTIL.   BR.

STUDIO   LAUN.   BR.

A SIMPLE SQUARE BOX ON A MOUNTAINSIDE

This vacation house is good evidence of the continuing use of inventive and playful forms in the design of weekend retreats. Low cost and compact, it uses maintenance-free natural materials. Located on a rugged mountain site and oriented to take advantage of an impressive view to the west, this simple and compact weekend house was designed for both summer and winter use. All openings are deeply carved to form roof overhangs for protection from heavy snow. Steps to elevated decks provide easy access at any snow depth in winter. During the summer, the doors and windows open to the decks and the breeze. Deeply setback porch with cantilevered deck provides additional summer living space, cross ventilation and an impressive view to the west. To create a structure compatible with its rugged site, the architect utilized straight-forward form with strong detailing—shed roof, reverse board and batten siding, and cantilevered decks with heavy railing seats. The house has a compact plan basically divided into a sleeping zone and a living zone, separated by the service core. Two other considerations affected the design: a tight budget ($16,000 in 1967 with unfinished basement and exclusive of furnishings); and minimum maintenance as reflected in the materials used—interior wood ceilings, exterior redwood siding, and use of stains for trim.

Architect and *owner:* Andrew Daland. *Location:* West Bethel, Maine. *Contractor:* Grover & Jordan, Inc.

1978: $36,000

"Hey, what's going on up there!"

Chapter Four:

SITE-DETERMINED SOLUTIONS

Introduction

Nowhere is the difference between an architect-designed house and a developer-built house more apparent than in site planning. Many a developer's primary site-planning tool is the bulldozer. With it, trees are toppled, hills flattened, and a swath of topsoil removed, all the better to obtain clear access to the building sites for trucks, cement mixers, and the like. When the buyers of these houses take possession and begin to think about their yards, they are faced (with luck) with a few trees and mounds of clay, drainage problems, and years of planting and work ahead. The advent of environmental impact statements has changed this all too little as yet.

Contrast this to the site plan of the first house in this chapter. The drive from the street to the Leader house (p. 56) curves gently yet sharply enough so that the occupants of the house can neither see nor be seen from the street. The basic plan of the house is a "C" shape around a tree. The living room is placed at the highest level, so that the owner can look at the church spires and lights of the village.

Each of the other houses in this chapter is a special case in which the relationship of the site to the house is the primary consideration. The Mark house (p. 58) steps down into a glacial basin to combine privacy with a view. The Chiu residence (p. 60) site plan inserts a house into a sloping lot, masking it with trees and minimally affecting the natural features of the site. An old stone fence provides a retaining wall for the Maxey house (p.62).

Two houses in this chapter show what can be done with really difficult sites: the Campbell house (p. 70) is built on a steep, small (60 x 80 foot) lot. The Fowler house (p. 74) is set diagonally on its flat site to provide good views of the only visually exciting land feature.

Since land costs have skyrocketed in recent years, it seems logical to control house costs by utilizing less desirable (from a developer's viewpoint) sites for affordable architect-designed houses. Such sites might be steep, or narrow, or have poor access. Natural drainage may be poor, or bedrock may be near the surface. Despite their low cost, undesirable-to-developer sites often provide good views and drama for houses when handled by architects. Moral: look for cheap sites!

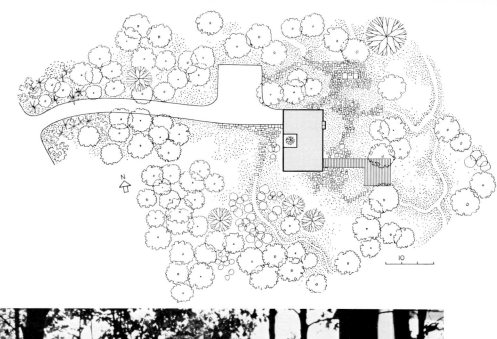

Robert L. Rotner

Architect Rotner's client, Robert Leader, wanted to sit on his terrace in the early evening and gaze upon the church spires of the village. At night he hoped to see the lights of the town. His heavily wooded site, however, offered no vistas, and it soon became clear that the living quarters of the house should perch in the treetops. To find the best elevation for town viewing, Rotner and Leader climbed a few trees and decided the higher the better.

To achieve as much elevation as possible, the house was designed on four levels as the section indicates. Five steps down from the entrance level are the bedrooms and garage and eleven steps up are the kitchen-dining area and the library. Opening off the dining area is a bridge leading to a small dining terrace (opposite page, right). At the top of the last flight of stairs is the living room which at one end overlooks the kitchen so that the owner, who cooks, remains in touch with his guests. From the master bedroom at grade, a path leads to

a gazebo roofed by the dining terrace.

The house has been designed for a bachelor with resale value in mind. It is essentially a three-bedroom, two-bathroom house suitable for a small family, but the bedrooms are so located that one serves Leader conveniently as a combined library and guest bedroom and the other as a combined office and guest bedroom.

The scheme provides a lot of privacy for a house so small. The sleeping areas are neither underneath nor adjacent to the living room, allowing those who choose peace and quiet to get away from a party. The extended porch with gazebo below economically increases the dimensions of the house and intensifies its relationship to the outdoors.

The house is of wood frame construction with tongue and groove cedar on plywood sheathing. It was built by Hal Young General Construction Co. for approximately $26 per square foot in 1970-71, for a total of $52,000.

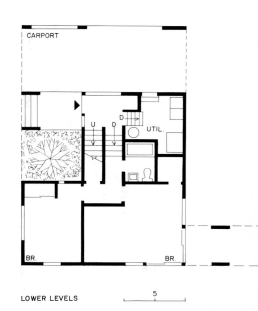

LOWER LEVELS

1978: $45/sq. ft.

James Brett photos except where noted

Robert L. Rotner

Robert L. Rotner

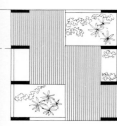

L.R.

OPEN

KIT.

U

D

LIBRARY   D.R.

UPPER LEVELS

A

A

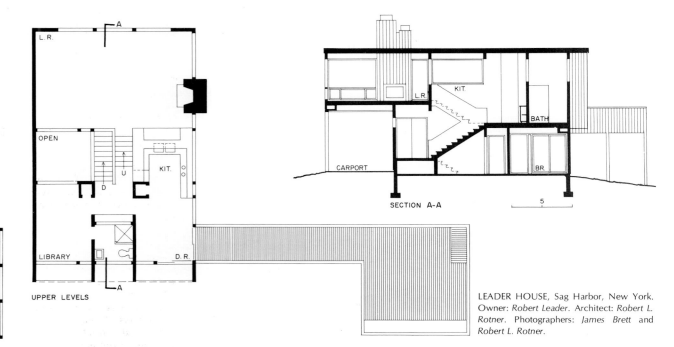

SECTION A-A

L.R.

KIT.

BATH

CARPORT

BR.

5

LEADER HOUSE, Sag Harbor, New York. Owner: *Robert Leader*. Architect: *Robert L. Rotner*. Photographers: *James Brett* and *Robert L. Rotner*.

Steve Rosenthal photos

TREE-HOUSE, FAMILY SIZE

Truro is a small community located near the northern tip of Cape Cod. The peninsula narrows abruptly near Truro to a minimum width of half a mile, granting many residents views of both the ocean and the bay. The land is tufted with scrub pine and pocked by small glacial basins.

This summer house for a minister and his family, designed by architect Paul Krueger, stands at the lip of one such basin and steps down into its depth to provide a measure of privacy for the lower level bedroom. A twelve-foot-wide, three-level volume, the house is framed in tripled 2 by 12s diagonally braced at top and bottom. Additional bracing—against high winds—is provided by external guy wires turnbuckled to "dead men" at either side of the house (see photo above).

Built on an extraordinarily modest construction budget, the house is clad in cedar board and batten, exposed on the exterior, and joined to the main vertical structure by horizontal nailers. Floors are fir decking and the roof is finished in cedar shingle. Minimum enclosure, simple construction, minor requirements for equipment, and the sparing use of interior finishes kept costs at rock bottom. But in spite of these economies, the Mark house has a freshness and inventiveness that derives from its siting and the playfulness of its forms. The interior spaces open outward and upward to expand the 12-foot-width and provide easy avenues of visual release. Inside and out, the house has a consistent vocabulary of de-

tails and a pleasant sense of leisure and relaxed informality. It is a house where wet bathing suits do not seem out of place.

Future plans include a small bedroom wing to be constructed farther down the slope and attached to the main structure by a stepped bridge. When the addition is complete, the existing lower level bedroom will become a family room.

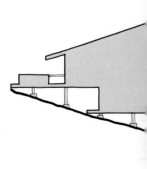

Architect: Paul H. Krueger. *Associate architect:* Malcolm Montague Davis. *Owner:* Reverend and Mrs. Edward L. Mark. *Location:* Truro, Massachusetts. *Structural engineers:* Tsaing Engineering; *structural consultant:* Souza and True. *Contractor:* Colp Brothers.

1978: $20,400

The approach to the house is a 12-foot-wide bridge-deck that provides a pleasant, sequestered setting for outdoor dining. It also introduces a design theme that will be expanded when the planned bedroom wing is added farther down the basin.

The architect had hoped to expose the braced structure over the roof but was barred from doing so by local code.

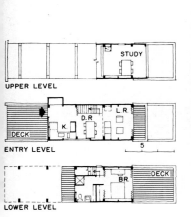

STUDY

UPPER LEVEL

DECK | K. | D.R | L.R

ENTRY LEVEL

BR | DECK

LOWER LEVEL

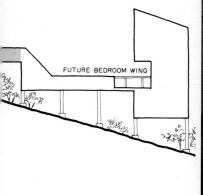

FUTURE BEDROOM WING

Chiu residence
Vancouver, British Columbia
James K. M. Cheng, Architect

This 90- by 120-foot lot in a suburb of Vancouver is bounded by a street to the north, existing houses to the east and west and a pocket of city-owned parkland to the south. Architect Cheng's task was to insert a house for a family of four into the sloping site, disturbing the terrain and its natural growth as little as possible while maintaining the privacy its thick tree cover promised. The exterior photos suggest how successfully the house was positioned and masked by existing trees.

The plan is simple and unforced. The entry and secondary spaces are aligned along the largely closed north side. The principal spaces open to the south—to views of the parkland and to the city skyline beyond. Upstairs, the master bedroom at the east of the house is linked to the western bedrooms by a bridge that overlooks the double-height living room. A large skylight over the bridge balances the light from the large window openings in the living room. The decks extend the house southward toward the view and their 45 degree cutoff reflects the line of sight to neighbors at the west. The quarter turn of the masonry chimney stack diminishes its apparent mass and projects these 45 degree angles into the vertical plane.

The exteriors are finished in 1- by 4-inch resawn cedar boards applied vertically over a conventional platform frame. The same material is used inside for ceilings. The floors are oil-rubbed oak strip and match the exposed laminated beams, window trim and fireplace lintel. Most of the partitions are finished in gypsum board painted white to catch the shifting shadow patterns and brighten the interiors on dark Vancouver days. Artificial lighting includes both adjustable and recessed fixtures, both types located to augment the natural light.

The inherent modesty of the house, its design subtleties and careful detailing notwithstanding, kept costs moderate. It was built for about $30 per square foot without land, fees and furnishing.

Architect: James K. M. Cheng
  1345 Laburnum Street
  Vancouver, B.C.
Owner: Mr. & Mrs. Stephen Chiu
Engineer:
  A. Robert Taylor (mechanical)
Contractor: Cervenka Construction
Photographer: James K. M. Cheng

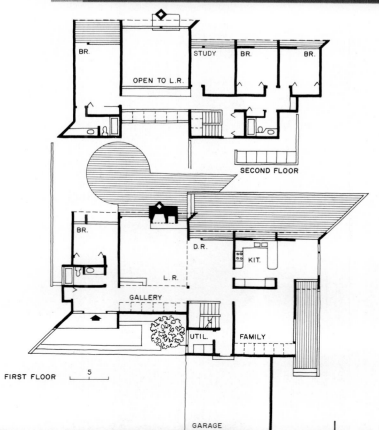

BR.

OPEN TO L.R.

STUDY   BR.   BR.

SECOND FLOOR

BR.

D.R.

KIT.

L.R.

GALLERY

UTIL.   FAMILY

FIRST FLOOR   5

GARAGE

Maxey residence
Wayne County, Pennsylvania
Lyman S.A. Perry, Architect

A Philadelphia lawyer and his family commissioned Lyman Perry to plan this house for their vacation and weekend use. The open-field site slopes sharply to the south and east offering, as it does so, expansive views of the Upper Delaware Valley. An old stone fence, neglected and crumbling, cut east-west across a portion of the hillside. Perry had the fence rebuilt and generated the stepped section of the house by using a portion of the fence as a retaining wall. The expanded saltbox forms are a response to its rural setting, its modest budget, and the requirement to throw off snow in a region of severe winter storms.

The plan is tightly organized around the two intersecting axes of circulation. The lower levels contain living room and kitchen as well as two bedrooms and bath. Bedrooms and a small study occupy the upper level and the upstairs circulation space overlooks the living room (photos below). Both upstairs and down, the circulation spaces are terminated with large glazed openings that provide orienting views to site, fill the interiors with natural light, and are protected by sliding wood panels during inclement weather or when the house is not in use.

The structure is post-and-beam with tongue-and-groove cedar decking. For greater strength and added insulation the stud walls are framed in 2 x 6 members and clad in vertical cedar siding. Floors on the lower level are finished in quarry tile that runs a color range from red-brown to purple.

The Maxey house is a nice example of what can be accomplished on a controlled budget ($25 per square foot) by a designer sensitive to the site and to his client's needs. Not prepossessing, not polemical, not overly fussy, it re-arouses our interest in "timeless" forms and in the simplified lifestyle these forms have long expressed so persuasively.

Architect: Lyman S.A. Perry
  311 North Newton Street Road
  Newton Square, Pennsylvania
Owner: David W. Maxey
Engineers:
  Keast and Hood (structural)
Contractor: Norella Brothers
Photographer: Positive Two Studios

1978: $29/sq. ft.

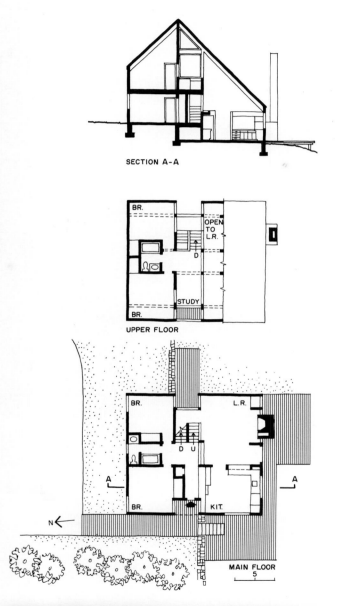

SECTION A-A

UPPER FLOOR

MAIN FLOOR

As the interior photos below clearly indicate, the spatial development of the house is vertical with overlooks and see-throughs used to emphasize this verticality. Not shown in plan is a detached, two-car garage with work shed.

A TWO-ZONE HOUSE THAT FOLLOWS THE SLOPE

Joseph Molitor photos

The Hunters have placed each wing on one of the two natural levels of the land. The connecting helix exactly follows the slope between the wings, as can be seen in the photograph on the left. For rental purposes the children's work area could convert to a kitchen. To get extra space in the summer the outside deck doubles as a dining area. A simple wood frame is articulated by exposing the interior posts and beams. Continuity between the interior and exterior is achieved by carrying the beams out to the overhang and minimizing the window framing. The simplicity and cleanness of design makes maintenance easy.

In designing this house with separate facilities for parents and children, E. H. and M. K. Hunter have also solved the problem of what to do with a large house after the children have gone away to school. Two separate wings linked by a helix-shaped hallway give the parents and children privacy. Eventually, the hallway can be closed off, creating two complete houses. Since only blank walls of the two wings face each other, privacy would be maintained.

Stone for the exposed foundation, pried from rocky ledges on the site, and rough-sawn redwood siding blend with the surrounding New Hampshire woods. Simplicity, an inherent characteristic of this house, is especially evident in the sensitively detailed and proportioned windows. The roof overhang and wall extensions sharply define the windows and shield the interior from sun.

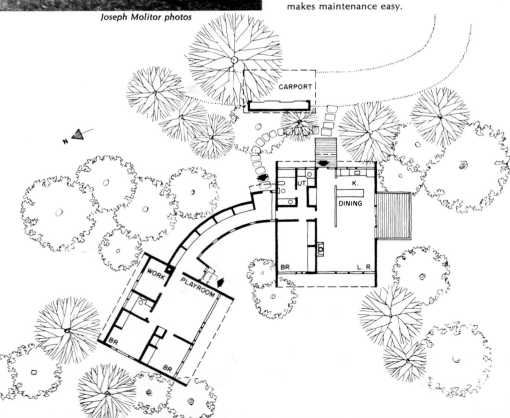

Interior details are handled with the same meticulous care as the exterior. The open plan of each wing appears large for a relatively small area. A prefabricated fireplace and chimney helped to save on construction costs, which were a major consideration. Although the house is quite modern, the clients' own tastes in furnishings seem to fit well. Yellow cabinets on an orange wall were used to brighten up the kitchen area.

Architects: E. H. and M. K. Hunter. *Owners:* Mr. and Mrs. Desmond Canavan. *Location:* Hanover, New Hampshire.

A TALL SHINGLE HOUSE IN A CALIFORNIA GROVE

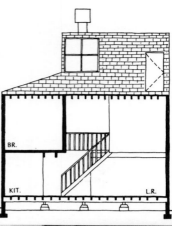

A three-story-high vertical living space transforms this simple-appearing, shingle-clad house into quarters for a very relaxed way of life. The architects state that "the owners had tired of their large conventional house, and were anxious to spend their limited budget on the excitement usually associated with a vacation house, rather than on the fixtures and appliances ordinarily expected in a house for year-round living." The resulting house thus minimizes "service" aspects (there is a wall-kitchen), and concentrates on a riot of color, space, comfort, books, music, and a balcony which serves as a quiet sitting nook, and occasionally as a stage for theatricals and a place to hold a band for parties.

The owners, Mr. and Mrs. Karas, are a couple whose children are grown. Thus "zoning" was not as important as in a house for a larger family; living space, in effect runs throughout the house, wheeling around the little service core on the first floor, and rising to the high shed roof. There are two principal bedrooms and a bath on the second level; on the third level is a loft, reached by a ladder, for visiting children.

Architects: Charles W. Moore and William Turnbull, Jr. of MLTW/Moore Turnbull. *Owners:* Mr. and Mrs. Sam Karas. *Location:* Berkeley, California. *Engineer:* Patrick Morreau of Davis & Morreau Associated; *Contractor:* Douglas S. Chandler.

OPEN

BR.

BR.

OPEN

SECOND FLOOR 5

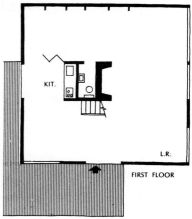

KIT.

L.R.

FIRST FLOOR

A "sun scoop" is employed in the Karas house to gain extra light on the pine-forested site, which is often foggy and sunless. Over one of the larger, upper windows in the living space, a "white baffle with an enormous yellow sun painted on it is enlisted to bounce south light into the house and to warm up the atmosphere within to a surprising degree", according to the architects.

A lower-ceilinged portion of the first floor living area is dominated by a large fireplace, which was cast in sand on the floor of the house by the contractor. This area has been treated as a smaller, cozier retreat, as contrasted with the taller reaches of other parts of the room. The furnishings of the house, many of which are built-in, are simple and sturdy, and rely for effect on bright splashes of color and a liberal sprinkling of handcraft accessories. As its original program has intended, the house does lend itself to a sort of perpetual vacation life—and in a remarkable and very different way.

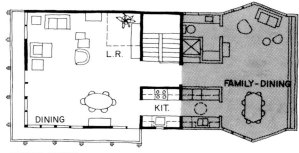

UPPER FLOOR

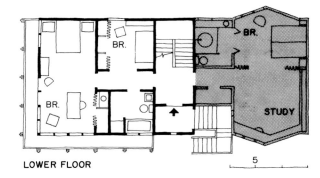

LOWER FLOOR

5

Karl H. Riek photos

The Campbell House

John Carden Campbell has used a great deal of ingenuity and skill in the design of this very attractive—and pleasantly unselfconscious—house for himself. The greatest problem, as well as the greatest asset, was presented by the lot itself. It is small (60 by 80 feet), steep, uphill and costly ($30,000 in the mid-1960s). But it has a most spectacular water view of San Francisco, many beautiful plum trees, and is in an excellent weather area.

Campbell has outlined his design objectives for a house on this site as follows: "1) to design a very economical house for a very expensive lot, which could be expanded later to justify the original land cost; 2) to make the greatest use of the view; 3) to get two cars and about 1400 square feet of house on the site without cutting the trees; and 4) in addition to these basic factors, it was desired to create a house whose interiors and the exterior were related to each other—to produce an integrated structure on a limited budget."

All these objectives have been handsomely achieved in the final house, which seems unusually spacious for the square footage, and which cost about $27,000 in 1966. In arriving at the three-level scheme, Campbell comments that, "after the cars are on the small lot, one must build over them to save land. For economy, the house is a box sitting on a carport. Also, because of the trees that were to be saved, and to get the most expansive view, the living room, kitchen and future dining room were placed on the top floor. The master bedroom has a good, though not as broad, bay view. And because of the size, the setbacks, the view, and the trees, the house is angled on the site and kept close to the street to leave room for expansion. To integrate the structure with the interiors, specially designed crystal-cut boards were used inside and out for walls, furniture, exterior rails and panels, the front door and even some picture frames."

Architect, interior designer, and owner: John Carden Campbell. *Location:* Sausalito, California. *Engineers:* William Gilbert of Gilbert, Forsberg, Diekmann & Smith. *Contractor:* John Sonne.

As the plan (page 29) shows, the Campbell house has been reduced to four rooms by combining functions: a large living-dining room, a compact kitchen, a large master bedroom and study, and a small second bedroom. The scheme permits future expansion to three bedrooms, two baths, dining room and upstairs toilet.

The great feeling of space in the house has been created, not only by using the same specially cut boards inside and out, but by all white interiors, the sense of extension given by the balconies, and the actual shapes and sizes of the rooms. The living room is 21 feet square, with 12-foot ceilings. The idea of unity is further carried out, as can be noted in the photo at left, by treating walls, cabinets and curtains in a consistent manner: The curtains are linen tapers, cut and hemstitched to match the two sizes of the boards, and the same striated pattern is seen inside and out. Yellow, orange and tile red are used as accent colors against the all-white background.

1978: $60,750

COMPLEX FORMS
FOR DRAMA
ON A FLAT SITE

"Overlapping sheds with skylight spaces between forms" is Clovis Heimsath's description of his design concept for this house, which was built in Houston for a sculptor and his family. A strictly limited budget and the requirement for two studios in addition to comfortable family living areas made this a challenging program for the architect. Mr. Heimsath solved the problems by adopting a shed roof motif which allowed sufficient height and volume for the creation of exciting two-story spaces and constantly changing patterns of light and shade inside and out.

Visual continuity of space between floors was very important since budget restrictions limited floor area, but a "row of little rooms" would have been functionally and esthetically unacceptable to the clients and the architect. The height was emphasized by strategically placed skylights which serve to extend the experience of space.

The first two-story space is the dramatic entry which is spanned by the hall on the second floor; the upstairs studio is a balcony above the sculpture studio on the lower level. The third two-story dimension is provided by the master bedroom which overlooks part of the living room.

The plan was developed around a central core, which consists of washer-dryer facilities and a powder room downstairs, two bathrooms above and necessary ductwork. The architect insists that this is where the scheme started. He says: "The design truly developed from plan to form. The clients had two children and might later add to the family, so the plan had to have three bedrooms, two studios, two and a half baths, living room and

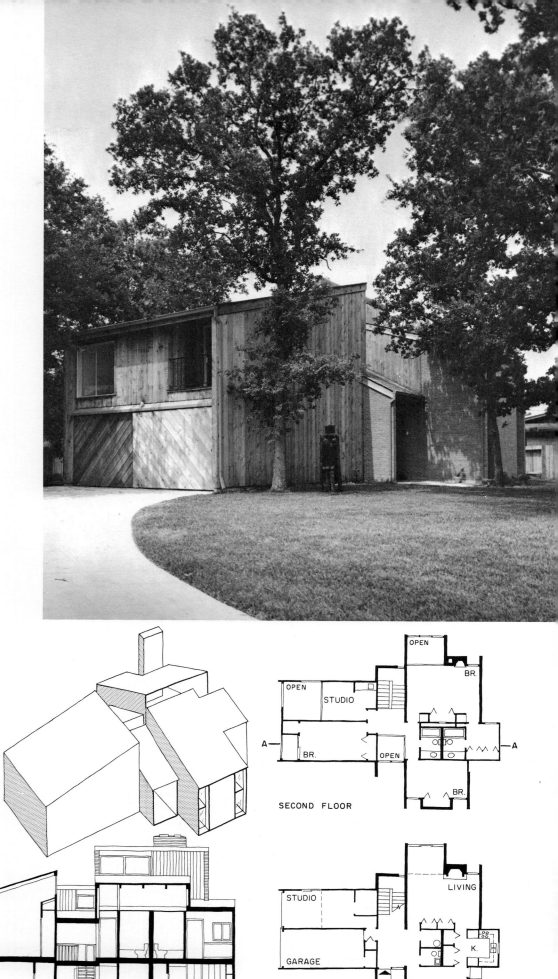

SECOND FLOOR

SECTION A-A

FIRST FLOOR

family-dining room. I started with the core and from there evolved a plan which placed the kitchen and family-dining room on one side, and the living room on the other. Upstairs the master bedroom and one other bedroom are separated by the bathrooms. The hallway had to be minimum, so the entry-stair hall relationship fell in place. It was at this point that the shed roof motif seemed appropriate to give me volumetric space, and to allow skylight spaces between the forms."

Mr. Heimsath says that he had some difficulty in deciding how to relate the studio wing with the rest of the house. The massing of the other forms built up into a "counter thrusting" relationship, but the studio wing had nothing to counter thrust against. It was therefore turned around "to play off against the rest of the house. Then it worked." The resulting scheme has a rather compact, sculptural effect, but the many skylights give it life and interest and save it from being too inward-looking.

Mr. Heimsath is convinced that no two rooms in one house should have the same spatial impact. By placing storage on the exterior wall of the family room— in contrast to the living room where it is on the interior wall, with the fireplace on the outside—he was able to vary the interior spaces and at the same time provide sufficient exterior massing to offset the dominance of the shed forms.

Architect: Clovis Heimsath; *Owner:* Mr. and Mrs. Robert K. Fowler, Jr.; *Location:* Houston; *Contractor:* W. A. Simmons

A certain amount of flexibility was provided by making the ground floor studio convertible to a garage if necessary, and the upstairs studio to a fourth bedroom if required. The house is set diagonally on its site, allowing a view up a bayou on one side. From the balcony of the children's bedroom above the garage, there is a pleasant outlook up the tree-lined street. Exterior materials of brick, rough-cedar and glass are well detailed and carefully related to each other.

"He broke the box alright—if that's any consolation."

Chapter Five:

HOUSES AS SCULPTURE

Introduction

As Alan Dunn's cartoon implies, the box has been the most popular shape for houses. No wonder, therefore, that Malvina Reynolds' popular song, *Little Boxes On A Hillside,* aroused so much self-deprecating laughter when we first heard it in the sixties. Strangely enough, the box shape, handled with skill, can produce attractive housing designs, as witness a number of boxy houses in this book.

However, the houses which follow are included because of their dramatically sculptured forms. Even when they are purely rectangular in form, such as the Lowenstein house (p. 80), surprises await the viewer in the form of light-and-shadow-revealed penetrations of the form. The DeSwaan house (p. 82), is described as a perforated box — and is unboxy because of its forward and trailing decks.

The addition of curved elements and a triangular loft gives the Moger house (p. 84) a distinctively sculptured form. A unique site problem — a spreading banyan tree — produced the unusual solution of the Weinberger house (p. 88), a concrete masonry house floating three feet off the ground.

Of the houses in this chapter, I think I like the Weinberger house best, although I'd like to try living in the Moger house.

This house has all the major attributes of a vacation house —plenty of light, pleasant views, closeness to nature, and privacy—although it is on a confined 65- by 62-foot lot within a crowded shore community.

It is very near the sea, two doors away, but has no direct access to it. Nevertheless, architect Louis Sauer has ingeniously captured views of the sea from the roof deck above the third-floor studio, from the studio through the skylight and from the second-story bridge through the living room windows (see section opposite). With no other way of relating to the sea and no desirable views into the neighborhood, the house turns toward the sky and inward, providing its own environment.

Its focus is the central, three-story-high, skylighted atrium (see plans) with a fish pond under the main stair and a bed of tropical plants under the skylight. At the second-story level the atrium is crossed by two bridges, one to the master bedroom, the other connecting the main stair and the children's rooms. From the latter bridge to the studio is a flying stair which, like the other stairs, has open risers. These elements, visually exciting themselves, form a network of viewing platforms. The main bridge overlooks the two-story living room (photo lower left, opposite). The only rooms which are isolated from the atrium are some bedrooms. The kitchen looks right into it over the snack bar (center photo opposite).

The large, second-story living room windows (photos above and opposite) have angled fins that deflect direct afternoon sun and block the view of houses from the bridge so only the sea and sky are visible. Beneath them is another private landscape—an indoor planter for tropical plants within a fenced outdoor garden of native plants. Windows in the rest of the house are minimal and mostly placed in corners or light scoops for privacy.

This $60,000 house has concrete block foundations, a wood frame structure, and cedar plywood siding. The pitched roof is lead painted orange.

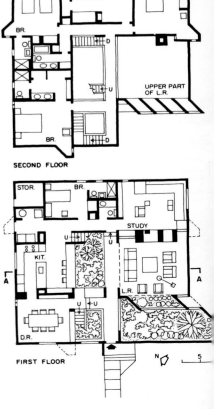

SECOND FLOOR

FIRST FLOOR

Architects: LOUIS SAUER ASSOCIATES, 2011 Chancellor Street, Philadelphia, Pennsylvania
Project architect: Terence L. Brown. *Project designer:* Cecil Baker
Owner: Mr. and Mrs. Leonard Frankel. *Location:* Margate, New Jersey
Mechanical engineer: Williams Eads of M. Michael Garber Associates
Structural engineer: Joseph Hoffmann; *Landscape architects:* Collins and Dutot Associates
Interior design: Susan Frankel Maxman; *Contractor:* E. J. Frankel Enterprises, Inc.

The complex volumes of this house are clad in gray cedar and outlined by bright, orange-painted, metal fascias, down-spouts and gutters. In the fire-place wall (photo below) between living room and study are several of many see-throughs. The area above the shoulders of the fireplace is open. The fire, the adjacent bar (left) and the TV, which swivels in a two-way nook (right), can be enjoyed from either room. A surprise interior window faces the flue.

Bill Maris photos, courtesy of House and Garden

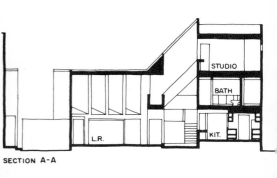

SECTION A-A

STUDIO

BATH

L.R.

KIT.

1978: $104,400

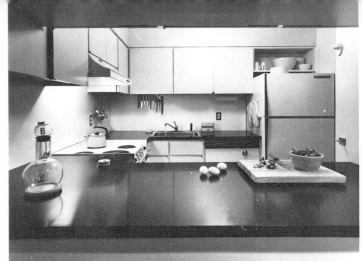

UPPER L.R.

BR

D

BR

DECK

L.R.

DINING

KIT.

D U

BR

ALUM. FLASH'G
5/8"

STOP FLASH'G

NEOPRENE SPONGE AT ALL VERT. JOINTS

1/2"

1/2"

Norman McGrath

This vacation house in eastern Long Island stands on a high point of ground surrounded by dense shrubbery and overlooking both the ocean and the town of Montauk. Both the owners, Mr. and Mrs. Peter Lowenstein, and the architects Chimacoff/Peterson, share a preference for simple geometric forms and neither wished to thrust aggressive shapes into this gentle landscape. The resulting design, therefore, is a simple prismatic volume of 900 square feet enclosed in a framework created by extending the exterior columns and joists to points of intersection. The larger

envelope embraces a deck, gives the whole composition an exciting transparency, and prints the solid walls with a changing abstract of cast shadows.

The south elevation (above) faces the ocean and will be fitted with adjustable canvas blinds to control the sun and glare. Just off the deck is a small grass plateau, formed by fill from the excavations, where badminton and volleyball are regularly played as part of the summer routine. At the open west end of the house (photo top), a series of observation and sunbathing platforms can be reached by

retractable ladders. Living, dining and kitchen areas share the deck level with a small guest room. A bath and two bedrooms—one overlooking the living area—occupy the upper level.

Standard materials and construction techniques have been used throughout. Exterior wall surfaces are painted plywood used, when possible, in full 4-by-8-foot sheets and put in place without battens but spaced apart by strips of flashing that give the narrow reveals a visual emphasis (see detail opposite page). Construction costs for this house were just under $40,000.

What is most appealing about the Lowenstein house is the degree of interest and spatial liveliness it generates within a carefully ordered and economic building system. Also noteworthy is the rapport the architects have established between house and site, a rapport that results from a conscious effort to place two different elements in amicable contrast.
Architects: CHIMACOFF/PETERSON. *Owner:* Mr. and Mrs. Peter Lowenstein. *Location:* Montauk, Long Island, New York. *Structural consultant:* Donald P. Greenberg. *Contractor:* David Webb.

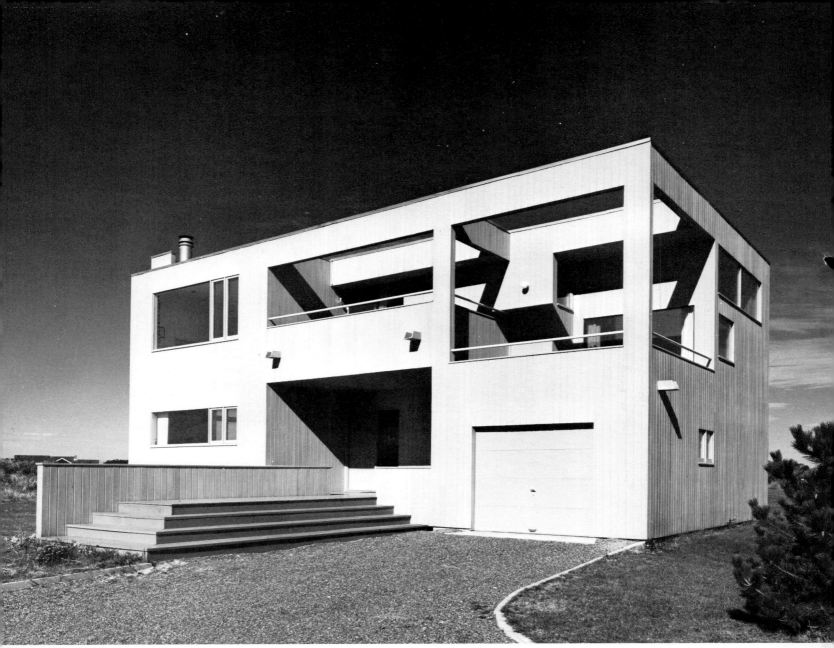

Client Sol de Swaan owns a full acre site in the rapidly disappearing Bridgehampton, Long Island potato fields. Although it doesn't front on the ocean, it has an ocean view. De Swaan's budget was $55,000 and his house cost approximately $26 per square foot in 1972-73. It is almost identical in size and materials to the Robert Leader house, but quite different spatially, because of differences in family requirements and site.

Unlike the Leader and Burke houses which are bachelor residences primarily, although they can be transformed for family use, the de Swaan house was designed from the beginning for a young family with one child. And unlike the Leader house, which is hidden in the woods, the de Swaan house is highly visible from all four sides and demands by its placement to be treated as a work of sculpture in the round. As such, it is highly successful, even though basically it is merely a humble box as the photo indicates.

The view from the living room is to the rear, over the potato fields and the terrace deck is located on this side. The house has four additional decks—one at the entrance and three which adjoin upstairs bedrooms. Each deck has several exposures and two overlook the ocean; all are partially shaded.

The garage is at grade and four steps above is the living-dining and utility area. Bedrooms, bathrooms, storage and decks occupy the remaining two levels as can be seen in the plans and sections.

The house is finished with red cedar tongue and groove siding over plywood sheathing on the exterior and the identical siding is used throughout the interiors. In all of his houses, architect Rotner uses standard metal kitchen cabinets framed in wood giving his kitchen installations a custom look. The interior furnishings of this house were selected by the architect. The contractor was Sag Hill Builders, Inc.

1978: $45/sq. ft.

Mildred F. Schmertz

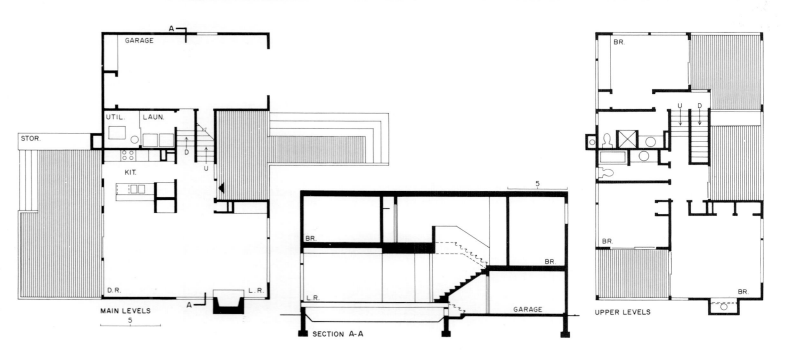

MAIN LEVELS

5

SECTION A-A

5

UPPER LEVELS

GARAGE

UTIL.   LAUN.

STOR.

KIT.

D.R.   L.R.

BR.

BR.

L.R.   GARAGE

BR.

BR.

BR.

BR.

Gil Amiaga photos

STRONG GEOMETRIC SHAPES AMIDST SHADOW AND SHADE

In this weekend and vacation house, architect Richard Moger displays as much skill in creating distinctive architecture with minimal size and budget as he has previously shown with more ample resources.

Though the house itself contains only 1500 square feet, and was built for $35,000, an illusion of far greater size—even luxury—has been created by some intriguing design techniques. The most obvious ones are the use of a modified "open plan," and the allocation of the greater part of the house to a big living room and minimal (but ample) spaces for other areas. These ideas, of course, have been around for quite a while, but here they have been combined with a highly successful interplay of scale,

light, openness and seclusion, which gives the sense of variety so often tragically lacking in a small house. In addition, Moger has incorporated an eye-catching *leitmotif* of rectangles and curves, all tied together by highly accented diagonal focal points; this, in the best sense, is the "decorative" element in the house—very simple, very architectural, with no frills, fuss or ostentation—and is obvious in the structure, the furnishings, even the wall hangings. This visual use of the diagonal (as can readily be seen in the photographs) increases the perspective and sense of visual space to a remarkable degree.

Though, when all doors are open, one can see—or at least be conscious of—most all of the spaces in the house

(and all these spaces somehow take advantage of the big, east-facing glass wall of the living area), necessary privacy is assured by doors to bedroom, baths, kitchen, and tracks provided for curtains, if they are desired, at the windows.

In part, the budget was met by simple construction: a wood frame on concrete block foundation, cedar siding, painted gypsum board interiors, built-up roof, quarry tile floors, furnace in outside-access crawl space. All is neat, easy to maintain.

Architect and owner: Richard R. Moger. *Location:* Southampton, New York. *Engineers:* Langer & Polise (mechanical); Paul Gugliotta (structural). *Contractor:* John Caramagna.

1978: $59,500

Basically rectangular in shape, the house gains character by some simply achieved, but highly rhythmical undulations of walls to express the activity areas and functions occurring inside. The combined sense of shelter and openness that occurs within is also expressed in the relatively closed entrance facade (across-page), the glass at back (far left and below).

Details throughout are simple, unobtrusive, well proportioned, with spaces and massing given importance; even on a limited budget, there is no deference to the "expose all the working innards" school—the mechanics of the house are not seen.

BALLENTINE HOUSE

ATLANTIC BEACH
FLORIDA

A vigorous interplay of spaces on five different levels in this modest-sized house, set four-square in a clearing of dense woods, makes a delightful environment for the varied activities of a suburban Florida family.

Rooms are organized around a central stair off a high foyer that reaches, like a core of space to the full 16-foot height of the house. By arranging the rooms spiral-fashion, the architect not only has brought related functions close together, but has created a play of levels that zones activities and gives to each area its unique spatial character. A great degree of privacy is also provided in an overall flow of space. The foyer is accessible from both formal entrance and carport. The stair quickly links the two major levels (shown in blue tint in the plans at right), the first of which—kitchen, dining and family rooms —is on the ground floor. Both kitchen and family room open onto the patio (below right), providing a center for the activities of two preschool daughters that is easily supervised by their mother. Passing a little conversation cove tucked behind the fireplace, one ascends four feet to a light and spacious living room. Returning to the central stair, one may reach a bridge over the foyer that links the upstairs bedrooms. Also on this level, a study balcony opens with folding screens back upon the living room and its broad window expanse. A sundeck is set into the roof over the firecove and provides a bonus "fun" space.

The Ballentine house is of simple pine post and beam construction. This, as well as the fir plywood siding and pine floor and roof decking are left exposed. For all its complexity of spaces, the house was easily framed, and the simple construction kept the cost to a moderate $35,000.

Architect: William Morgan, 1611 Ocean Boulevard, Atlantic Beach, Florida. Contractor: Ross Construction Co.: landscape architect and interior designer: William Morgan.

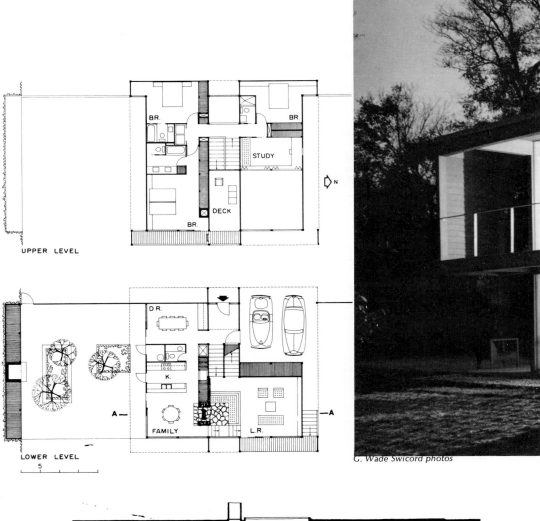

UPPER LEVEL

LOWER LEVEL

G. Wade Swicord photos

SECTION A-A

In contrast to a formal entrance facade, closed to the west in protection from a hot, tropical sun, the east elevation opens wide to offer all the major living areas a panoramic view of the encircling jungle. Four-foot-wide decks provide shade. At night, when the interior is ablaze with light, the boldly sculptural quality of the house is dramatized, with the overhangs reflecting as they do the strongly articulated structure and play of levels within. The view to the right is from the study balcony on to the living room and firecove. Trim built-ins and precise detailing of warm, natural-finished woods emphasize the interior's uncluttered play of intersecting planes.

Joseph W. Molitor photos

A major factor in the design problems of the house was the big banyan tree shown in the sketch at left (the tree is impossible to photograph—edges of it appear in the two photos here). The plan contains few but good-sized rooms. The child's room is divisible.

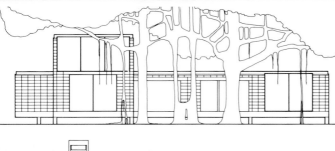

STUDIO   BR.

K.

L.R.   BR.

5

A WHITE SCULPTURE
IN A TROPICAL FOREST

"Like a big sculpture perched alone in a rain forest" is architect Singer's comment on this very interesting house he has designed for builder Lewis Weinberger. It is an apt analogy, for the trim concrete and concrete block forms do stand in sharp and sympathetic contrast to the site—part of a tract previously used as a nursery and now overgrown with such lush tropical vegetation as an 80-foot spreading banyan tree. Singer adds: "The shelter of that tree was desirable, but its root structure is devastating to anything resting on or within three feet of the surface of the earth."

"The solution to this was a foundation system designed as a series of short columns penetrating the root system and bearing on concrete pads poured below the problem level. Thus the masonry house floats serenely three feet off the ground."

The house is also well-geared to its tropical setting in other ways: tall rooms, cool and easy-to-keep surfaces, and an electric heat pump for year-round air conditioning.

In all floor, wall and roof systems used in the house, the structural material also provides the finish. Concrete beams span the distance between the foundation posts and carry precast floor joists which were set in the formwork of the beams; the flooring itself is of 2-foot-square reinforced-cement tiles.

All walls are concrete block, reinforced with concrete and steel. Precast concrete lintels span over openings to support the loads of the 4-inch laminated wood decking, which forms both roof and finished ceiling. Ductwork for the heating and air conditioning is carried to all areas of the house in a plenum over the hallway.

Architect: Donald Singer. *Owners:* Mr. and Mrs. Lewis Weinberger. *Location:* Miami, Florida. *Engineers:* Houha & Harry Associates. *Contractor:* Lewis Weinberger.

1978: $41,440

The living room (above and left) rises to a two-story height, and has a big clerestory window over the skylighted dining area. A little deck separates master bedroom (below) from the child's room.

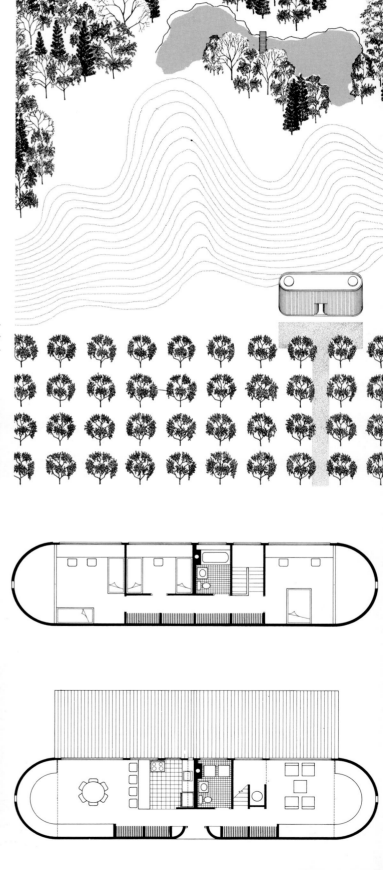

The important use of curved shapes in this house is to make it as abstract as possible—although in fact it is a simple, 14- by 70-foot winterized weekend and vacation house on the prairie in northwestern Illinois built within a $35,000 budget.

The important design idea is that the house is not four-sided, but two-sided—an idea established by the rounded ends divided by a louvered vertical strip on the centerline. And beyond that, the house is intended to be a series of oppositions or inversions. On the side facing the road (bottom in drawing, upper photo) the house is totally opaque and solid, with even the front door let in with curved shapes. Tigerman sees this side of the house as a performer on a stage, or as a proscenium, with an audience of apple trees to be planted 30 feet on center. The approach is deliberately not on axis—one is intended to see the house, then have it hidden behind the trees, enter the drive, "lose focus," and then unexpectedly come upon the house with no opportunity to study it or even know how big it is. Even its cedar wall is "an opposition" to the natural trees planted in a geometric (un-natural) way.

Once you enter the house and move to the living spaces, you are immediately "thrust out of it"—with glass walls in an (unnatural) Mondrian pattern overlooking a section of the site that slopes down to a swimming pond and huge old trees beyond.

Functionally, the glass wall reflects the simple plan behind: The tall window lights the stair well, the small window adjacent is over the tub, the larger windows open to bedrooms on the upper level, dining and living spaces below. Guests sleep on curved built-in couches on the main level.

The Hot Dog House (as it is inevitably known) has 1,600 square feet of living space, for a cost of $22 per square foot.

PRIVATE RESIDENCE, northwestern Illinois. Architects: *Stanley Tigerman & Associates.* Contractor: *Donald Zimmerman.*

Philip Turner photos

1978: $45,500

"And this is our—ah—picture window."

Chapter Six:

WITH A VIEW IN MIND

Introduction

A view! Trees, fields, mountains, streams, shores, anything goes, as long as it's not one's next door neighbors. Yet the desire for a view often goes along with the desire for privacy as well, and aside from one-way mirrors, this is not always possible. In one house I've recently seen, the master bedroom offers an unobstructed view — with privacy — day and night: there's a five-by-eight-foot skylight!

If you're lucky enough to find land with a view, and certain that the view can't be obstructed by someone else who likes it, by all means make that view — or views — part of the site planning for your house.

One important consideration should be *where* you're going to enjoy your view. Will it be the living room area, or would you prefer to enjoy the view from a deck area? Remember that it will require large areas of glass.

Homes in this chapter offer views from both, sometimes in the same house. In the Whisnant house (p. 96), views from the back of the house reveal the wooded hillside, while views from other sides are restricted to afford privacy.

Mountain *and* lake views are designed into the Meilleur house (p. 98), while the Adams house (p. 102), shows careful framing of its view possibilities while still affording the owners the privacy they desire.

Notice that none of these houses goes overboard in presenting a view of the occupants. You'll see no glass walls here. That's because too much of a good thing is as bad as too little — and living in a goldfish bowl can be just as disturbing as living with no windows at all.

Don't write off a site because only part of the view is attractive — careful siting of the house and framing of the view can do wonders for such a site. Finally, don't despair because you can't find a view site. In a subsequent chapter, we'll look at houses which create their own views.

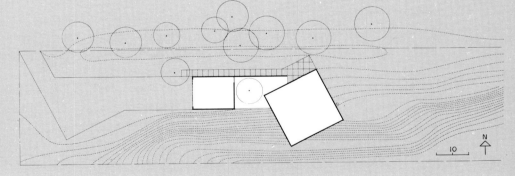

On a lot only 66 feet wide and sloping steeply to the south and west, architects Booth & Nagle designed this "cube" house for a doctor and his family in Des Moines, Iowa. The garage and entry wall parallel the contours but the main portion of the house is twisted 27½ degrees off this axis to take advantage of views to the garden and the ravine as well as to animate the simple massing. But even in the main house the contour axis is echoed in splayed partitions and non-rectilinear volumes.

The levels split at the entry: half a flight down to the kitchen, dining and living spaces; half a flight up to the master bedroom. Children's rooms and lounge occupy the uppermost level. Though a kind of zon-ing is clearly present, all these spaces inter-lock vertically as the plan opposite shows.

The simple forms of the exterior are restated inside but with functional compli-cations that add interest and visual enrich-ment. Color is used selectively but emphati-cally so that its design impact is not squan-dered. Nothing, in fact, is wasted. The fur-nishings are also selected carefully to achieve a sense of easy upkeep and pleas-ant understatement. The detailing is elegant but direct—a virtue consistent with the basic design goals.

The major materials are stucco for ex-terior finish, oak for flooring and trim, steel for sash and sliding door assemblies. The roof is built-up. Vertical glazing occurs at the corners of the house, a design device that washes white interior walls with day-light, giving the interior spaces an especially appealing quality of light.

Thanks to simple volumetric construc-tion and detailing and the sparing use of ex-pensive finishes, this exceptionally hand-some house was constructed for a quite moderate amount—the difficulty of the site notwithstanding.

1978: $28/sq. ft.

PRIVATE RESIDENCE, Des Moines, Iowa. Archi-tects: *Booth & Nagle—Marvin Ullman, job cap-tain.* Engineers: *Weisenger-Holland* (structural); *Wallace & Midgal, Inc.* (mechanical). Contrac-tor: *Byran Crow.*

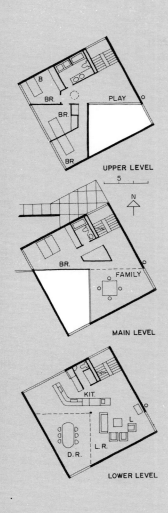

UPPER LEVEL

MAIN LEVEL

LOWER LEVEL

The architects have softened the effect of a determinedly angular scheme by introducing a gentle curve in the flow of cabinets around the partition that separates the kitchen and dining space (photos below). The contrast is unexpected but appropriate and pleasant.

Bill Hedrich, Hedrich-Blessing photos

A HOUSE AT ONCE MODEST AND MEMORABLE

This house for an architect and his family manifests common sense as well as talent, clear sightedness as well as imagination, practicality as well as dreams. The result is modest, clear and memorable—though it may take some readjustment of our expectations to perceive it, for what we are likely to remember is not an elegant architectural effect here or a striking detail there, or indeed even some dazzling form of the whole. What we will remember is a place made simply of simple materials, well-formed around the needs of the people who live there and attentive to the land on which it is built.

These qualities are not uncommon ideals in house design, and in fact most people would call them downright basic. In practice, though, they can easily get lost in the rush to achieve other more dazzling goals.

Architect and owner: Murray Whisnant. *Location:* Charlotte, North Carolina. *Engineers:* R. V. Wasdell & Associates (structural); J. M. McDowell & Associates (mechanical); S. T. Hocsak & Associates (electrical). *Contractor:* G. E. Vinroot Construction Company.

The main floor (drawing at right) is a series of rooms clustered around a central mechanical core that contains the kitchen and two baths. At one end of the plan are three bedrooms and at the other a large living and dining room that opens onto a cantilevered deck (large photo above); in front of the mechanical core is the entrance hall and behind is a small porch reached from either the master bedroom or the kitchen. On the lower level are an office (photo below right), a studio and a playroom.

The configuration of the suburban site and the placement of the buildings next door suggested that the house be relatively closed and viewless on the front and on one end (left photo below); accordingly the living room is lit on the front by a narrow band of windows just above eye level and by a sloping skylight in the ceiling (large photo opposite). At the back of the house (right photo below) the walls open up to provide a view down a wooded hill, both from the back porch and the living and dining room, and from the office below.

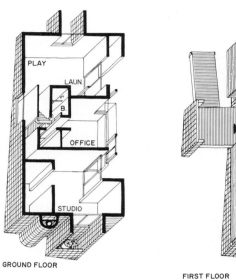

GROUND FLOOR

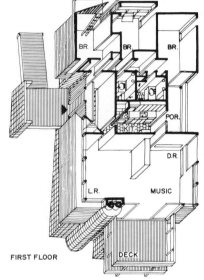

FIRST FLOOR

Gordon Schenk photos

Hugh N. Stratford photos

The strong shapes of this compact house closely echoes the site, and affords beautiful views of Lake Sammamish and the Cascade Mountains. As the setting is fairly open, the design of the house organizes solid walls and windows to give privacy from the road, openness to the view. The crisp, angular silhouette of the house is emphasized against the sky by the use of dark brown cedar siding, and copper for flashing and entrance roof.

The interior spaces are arranged on three levels: a raised basement, the main floor, and a partial second floor. The entry which is midway between the basement and main-floor levels, is actually a landing of the open stair constructed of steel and laminated wood. The basement was designed to provide a two-car garage, furnace room, recreation room, study/guest room, bath and darkroom. The top floor contains bedrooms and bath for two sons.

The main floor of the house has a spaciousness not readily apparent from the exterior. The living room is a large one, with a ceiling of suspended cedar paneling that follows the slope of the roof to a maximum height of 14 feet. A window wall and balcony open the space fully to the view. A low-ceilinged dining space is separated from the living area by a freestanding fireplace, yet the rooms are strongly tied together by a floor of red quarry tile—which covers all the main floor except for the carpeted master bedroom. A compact kitchen, with an adjoining laundry room, is placed between the dining area and the entrance stairs for convenience to all parts of the house.

Architect: WENDELL H. LOVETT
Owners: Mr. and Mrs. Peter Meilleur
Location: Bellevue, Washington
Mechanical engineer: Richard Stern
Landscape architects: Richard Haag Associates
Contractor: Pacific Northwest Construction Co.

BALCONY LEVEL
455 SQ. FT.

1978: $51,000

FIRST FLOOR
1323 SQ. FT.

98

The openness of the living-dining and entrance areas of the house is further extended by using a balcony as hallway to the upper-level bedrooms (photo, near right). The structure of the house is wood frame, surfaced with oil-stained red cedar on the exterior, painted plasterboard on the interiors. Aluminum sash is used throughout. Furnace and water heater are both gas fired. The master bath is compartmented, and its counter is tiled in Venetian glass.

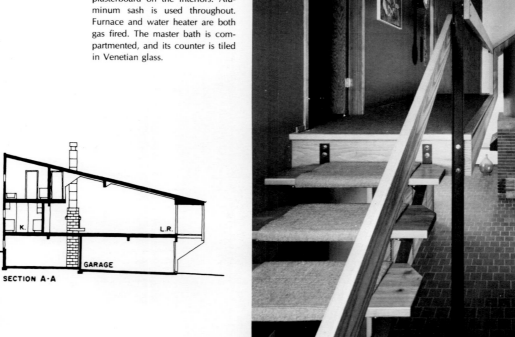

Christian Staub photos

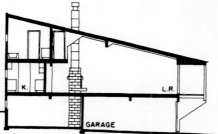

SECTION A-A

LeBOVIT HOUSE

McLEAN VIRGINIA

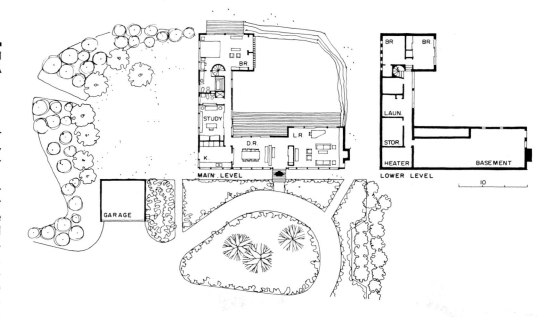

MAIN LEVEL

LOWER LEVEL

Calm sophistication is exemplified in this house, with its simple, comfortable blend of contemporary fashion and tradition.

Shed roofs, with their attendant angularly dramatic interior spaces, crisp, black-trimmed, white exteriors, and a kitchen arranged and placed for maximum convenience, are all in the latest idiom. Coupled with these are a lot of elegant, traditional formalities: the sweep of a carefully landscaped entrance drive; a sort of mini-version of an in-line, European "palace plan"; the second-level "main floor" (created by the ground slope); balconies for the main rooms; and the ready combination of major rooms and terraces for entertaining (even the guest bedroom, which can double as a library, has a sliding wall to join it with the hall and living areas).

The interiors are handled with the same simple restraint as the structure. White-painted, plasterboard interior walls echo the stucco exteriors, and serve as a bright foil for the strip-oak and hemlock flooring used respectively as floors and ceilings in the main rooms. Furnishings are a spare, well-placed mingling of old and new. The house is air-conditioned.

Reasonable economy was a key design factor (the budget for the house and garage was $48,000). Simplicity of structure and materials were the key factors in keeping within the cost limits. The frame is fairly standard 2 x 6 fir studs, and 2 x 10 joists and rafters form the shed roofs of the two wings. The lower level is painted concrete block. An unfinished basement area extends under the living room wing and can provide future bedrooms if, and where desired.

Architects: Joseph A. Wilkes and Winthrop W. Faulkner of Wilkes and Faulkner Architects, 1834 Jefferson Place, N.W., Washington, D.C. Owners: Mr. and Mrs. Harry LeBovit; engineer: James M. Cutts: contractor: Norris S. Wilson; landscape, interiors: Wilkes and Faulkner.

The L-shaped plan of this extremely pleasant house was designed to capitalize on two major views: one of the Potomac River from the living room wing, and one of a 150-foot-long, dramatic rock outcropping from the other. A landscape plan will be carried out to complement the site, with banks of dogwood and hollies, and an ivy-edged terrace developed for the lower level.

The owner is an amateur musician, and as a hobby makes violins of excellent quality; a special case is provided in the entrance hall for their display (photo at left).

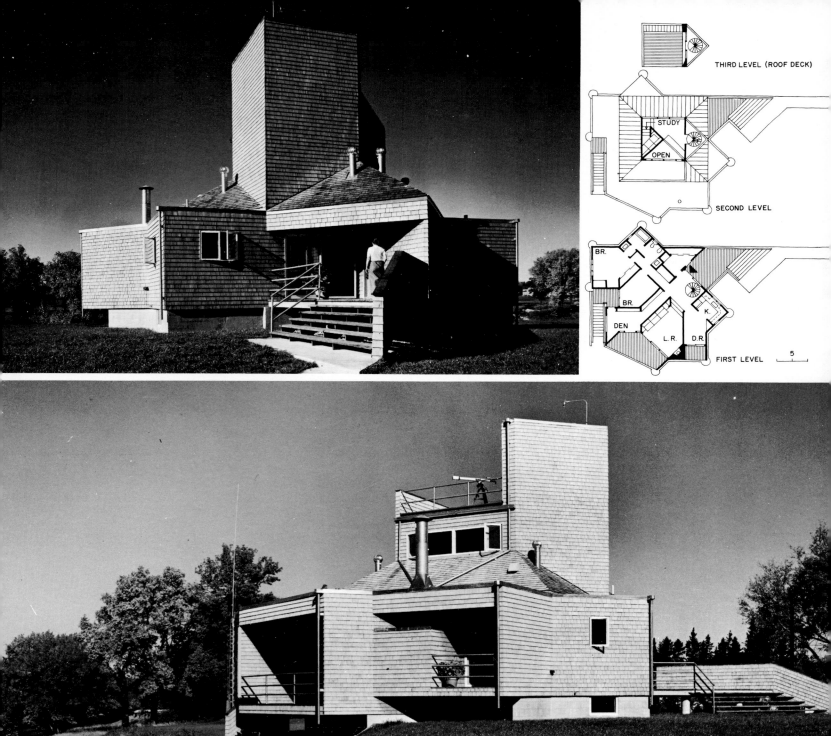

THIRD LEVEL (ROOF DECK)

SECOND LEVEL

FIRST LEVEL

Rugged and angular in character, this small year-round house for a newspaper editor and his wife is located in Roseau, Minnesota, just below the Canadian border. The triangular site fronts on a stream and opens toward the west to unobstructed views of a golf course beyond. The owners, Mr. & Mrs. William Adams, wanted privacy—within and without—and stressed their desire for a house that was spatially exciting and individualistic.

Architect Thomas Larson developed internal privacy by careful zoning (see plan) and augmented this feeling through the use of level changes, small niches and a two-foot-high parapet in the living room. The plan contains two unusual components: a private sun bathing platform on the roof and a mud room at the entrance—a practical necessity for climate control in a region where winter temperatures sometimes drop to 30 degrees below zero.

Framed in wood stud and sheathed in plywood, the Adams house is heated by forced air and insulated with double thickness of glass fiber batts. On wall and roof surfaces, the exterior finish material is red cedar shingle.

The unexpected complication of shapes give the plan a somewhat willful character, but the spaces seem to work well and flow together convincingly. The broken planes and angular development of the elevations aptly reflect the irregular interior volumes. The interesting assortment of roof vents, stove pipes, downspouts, rain leaders and whip antenna gives the house a pleasantly unedited appearance and suggests that architect and owners share a happy unconcern for self-conscious design as well as a firm grasp of the exigencies of building and function.

ADAMS RESIDENCE, Roseau, Minnesota. Architect: *Thomas N. Larson—John Warren, assistant.* Engineers: *Michael Jolliffe* (structural); *Robert Fairbanks* (mechanical). Contractor: *Arthur Anderson.*

SECTION

Interior finish materials are cedar boards for ceilings, plasterboard for partitions and carpeting or sheet vinyl on all floors. Counters are covered in plastic laminate. Foundation walls are concrete block.

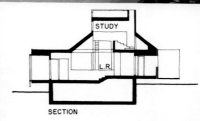

STUDY

L.R.

SECTION

Phokion Karas photos

1978: $67,510

A series of outdoor and indoor living spaces cascade dramatically down a 40-degree cliff to form this unusual, hospitable house. The half-acre plot is long and narrow (72 feet wide) and has mandatory setbacks of 20 feet on both sides, thus allowing a maximum house width of 32 feet. The program and other restrictions added further challenges: the budget was $40,000 for four bedrooms, two baths, living room, dining room, kitchen and ample outdoor space; local zoning dictated a maximum height of two and a half stories, but not to exceed 40 feet.

All this was organized into two linked, two-story units, with the upper one offset horizontally to allow a view of the Atlantic Ocean, and the lower unit stepped down the cliff one story. The offsetting of the units also gives the added benefits of a sheltered rear deck tucked in-

1978: $70,800

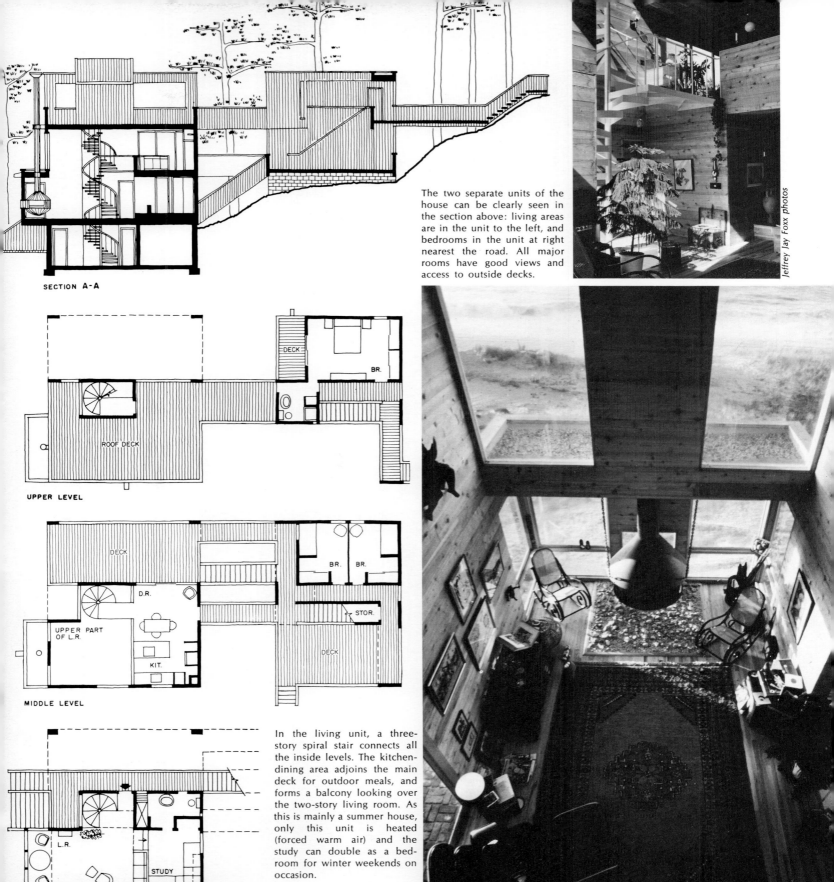

SECTION A-A

UPPER LEVEL

ROOF DECK

DECK

BR.

MIDDLE LEVEL

DECK

D.R.

UPPER PART OF L.R.

KIT.

BR. BR.

STOR.

DECK

LOWER LEVEL

L.R.

STUDY

5

Jeffrey Jay Foxx photos

The two separate units of the house can be clearly seen in the section above: living areas are in the unit to the left, and bedrooms in the unit at right nearest the road. All major rooms have good views and access to outside decks.

In the living unit, a three-story spiral stair connects all the inside levels. The kitchen-dining area adjoins the main deck for outdoor meals, and forms a balcony looking over the two-story living room. As this is mainly a summer house, only this unit is heated (forced warm air) and the study can double as a bedroom for winter weekends on occasion.

to the hill, a tall, canopy-shaded front deck overlooking the ocean, and easy access to the roof of the front unit for use as a sun deck. A series of stairs and bridges connect all parts of the house, inside and out.

Apart from its over-all impact, the most dramatic feature of the house is the two-story living room with its open fireplace set before double-glazed windows—one can view the fire and the ocean at the same time.

As local codes required a full foundation, the house was dug into the cliff, instead of being on wooden stilts as planned in preliminary stages. The basic structure is wood frame with exteriors of bleached cedar siding, and interiors of natural cedar; the materials are expected to weather well and to reduce future maintenance. There is 2,020 sq. ft. inside and 1,600 sq. ft. of deck.

Architect: RICHARD D. KAPLAN
150 East 52nd Street, New York City
Owners: Dr. William Lee Curry
Location: Montauk Point, Long Island
Engineer: Robert Sillman
Landscape architect: Richard D. Kaplan
Contractor: Jack Jackson

Chapter Seven:

RENOVATION AND RECYCLING

Introduction

There was a time, not too long ago, when you could renovate or rebuild a structure at rockbottom prices. Alas, those days seem to be gone forever. It is still true, however, that recycling is the least expensive way to achieve sizeable square footage.

With the exception of the Desberg house (p. 114), included in this chapter for its recycling of barn siding from a nearby structure, the houses which follow all feature large square footage living space. They range from a barn to a frame house, from a brick row house to two carriage houses, one of some 7,000 square feet!

Recycling appeals to many of us these days for many reasons besides cost, which as indicated is no longer the bargain-basement component of yore. We have come to appreciate Victorian architecture, for one thing, and the craze for tearing down old structures seems to be ending. At long last it has been recognized that the square footage enclosed by old buildings can be modernized to fit current lifestyles.

Having remodeled not one but two Victorian houses, I could spend weeks extolling their virtues and warning about their pitfalls. (Fortunately, space prevents that from occuring.)

Instead you are invited to inspect six renovated structures for yourself. Note that they range from minimal outside work in the Opp house (p. 112) to the all-but-totally-new outside of the Christiansen house (p. 108). None, however, is merely a reconstruction; each features a totally new interior arrangement and fully updated spaces.

Renovation has a lot going for it, when you consider that older buildings are often structurally sound, well-sited, and economically viable. They have another great advantage: you can frequently live in one portion while renovating another!

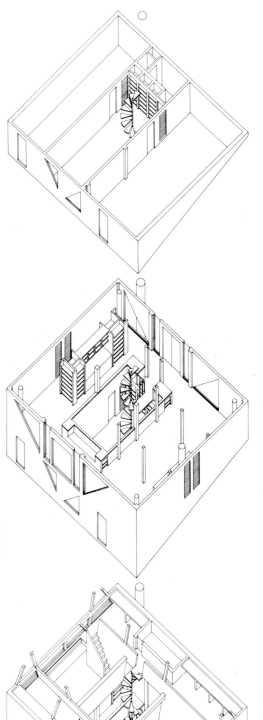

Take a gambrel roofed, Pennsylvania Dutch type barn, insert windows which make it smile like a Halloween pumpkin and wrap the whole thing in black asphalt shingles and what do you get? A form without precedent certainly, which some may consider a bit spooky. Others may feel it has a humorous presence rather like a figure in a Klee drawing. It is certain that the humble beasts which once inhabited this barn would never recognize their old home, but its present occupants—a veterinarian who is also an organist, his painter wife and their three children find that it suits them perfectly.

The plan includes a studio for the wife and accommodations for an organ. The scored plywood siding makes a handsome interior finish and provides a diaphragm structure which stiffens the 100-year-old barn. All conduit, heating ducts and plumbing are exposed and color-coded blue, red and yellow respectively. All glazing is gray-tinted plate. Costs were quite low, but the client does not wish to reveal them.

FROG HOLLOW, southern Michigan. Owners: *Dr. and Mrs. James Christiansen.* Architects: *Stanley Tigerman & Associates; associates—Anthony Saifuku and John Haley.* Engineers: *Raymond B. Beebe & Associates* (structural); *Wallace & Migdal* (mechanical and electrical). Interior design consultant: *Stanley Tigerman & Associates.* General contractor: *Lester & David Krumerie.* Principal subcontractors: *F. H. Klugh & Son* (mechanical); *Mead & White Electric* (electrical); *Ace Plumbing Co.* (plumbing).

Philip Turner photo

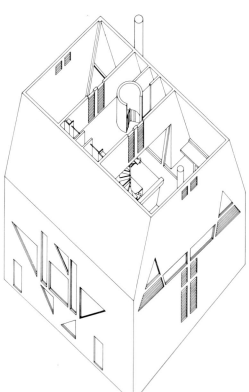

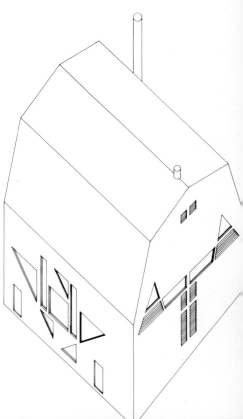

Balloon framing, an anonymous American invention of the early 19th century, has long been used for utilitarian buildings. Many older frame houses in small, older communities, are suitable for continuing usefulness. This house in the Hudson River community of Nyack is such a typical example. Built in the 1880s, it has now been remodeled to provide a residence and studio for a painter. All interior partitions were removed, and a new beam (two 2 by 12s bolted together) was put in on each level. Small columns were added at or near the two existing chimneys. Other changes included a new basement slab, new wiring, plumbing, and heating system. The exterior was largely unchanged. The basement level became studio, eating and cooking area. The front entrance, at the middle level, is adjacent to the unusual low-walled living room (opposite page, lower left) which overlooks the sitting area of the basement (below).

HOUSE AND STUDIO, Nyack, New York. Architect: *James R. Lamantia.* General contractor: *Kaplan Contracting Service.*

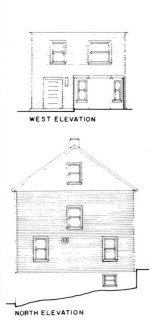

WEST ELEVATION

NORTH ELEVATION

Gil Amiaga photos

1978: $27,200

The old house was very simply converted at a cost of $16,000 into a comfortable, convenient and contemporary interior. The spacious living area and the ingenious opening of the living room to the rest of the house are notable features, as is the quality of each specific space.

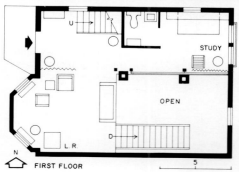

FIRST FLOOR

N

5

STUDY

OPEN

L.R.

U

D

SECOND FLOOR

ALCOVE

BR.

BR.

D

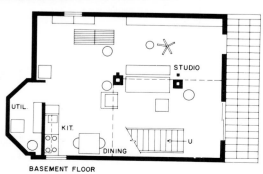

BASEMENT FLOOR

STUDIO

UTIL.

KIT.

DINING

U

Opp Residence
St. Paul, Minnesota
Design Consortium, Architects

An aging but still substantial brick rowhouse at the end of a residential block in St. Paul was the starting point for this elaborate residential renovation by the Design Consortium. Of the original interior, only the ornamental mantle, the stair to the upper level and the bathroom plumbing connections were retained. All else is new. The architects began by creating an upper and lower apartment, the lower making splendid use of what had been the 11-foot-high basement space (photo opposite). To make this basement volume fully habitable, the architects threw it open to the level above and borrowed light from the first floor windows. The result is a beautiful space keyed to all the other smaller spaces by carefully studied transitional elements. The delicacy of touch in this renovation is remarkable as is the intelligent use of color to reinforce the linear character of the design and the skillful development of secondary circulation on the raised gallery above.

The upper (entry) level provides a private bedroom at the rear, a more open bedroom overlooking the living room, and a private study reached by a warp in the line of the gallery (see photos).

The upper level apartment, when complete, will be a rental unit.

Renovated at a cost of about $24 p.s.f., the Opp residence is another superb reminder that re-use can produce important economies at no sacrifice to comfort or high visual impact.

Architects: Design Consortium
   1012 Marquette Avenue
   Minneapolis, Minnesota
   James Geisler, project architect
Owner: Roger Opp
Photographer: Phillip MacMillan James

1978: $24/sq. ft.

BR.

BR.

OPEN

STUDY

D

U

MAIN LEVEL
5

N

MECH.

LAUN.

D

D

KIT.

D.R.

U

U

L.R.

ST.

Desberg House
Central Ohio
Trout Architects, Inc.

In a rural Ohio setting—a small clearing partially masked by trees—Trout Architects designed this modest, year-round house, cladding it with siding recovered from a fallen barn nearby. The simple, vernacular quality of the exterior gives the house its appealing folk image, but the interior spatial development is considerably more complex. The main entry is at a mid-level solarium, a high, skylighted space filled with planting. Half a level below are the children's bedrooms and family room, while half a level above are the main living spaces. Half a level up again is the master bedroom suite. Above the bedroom is a small "retreat" (reached by a ship's ladder) that overlooks the living room. Spatial definition is apparent throughout the house but the volumes flow together through arched openings.

Finish materials have been selected for their ease of maintenance, and the detailing, though it is far from slapdash, heightens the sense of informality. Throughout the house, in fact, invention substitutes for visual refinement and the result is a design that is fresh and enriched with wit. The mirrored wall of the bathroom (photo below right) is fitted with a porthole that appears at first to be part of the mirror but it actually opens to an unexpected view of the roof trusses. The house is fully insulated and equipped with three fireplaces that augment a gas-fired heating system, keeping fuel bills down during the cold months of winter.

Architects: Trout Architects, Inc.
  19063 Lake Road
  Rocky River, Ohio
Owners: William and Karen Desberg
Engineer:
  Williams & Hach (structural)
Contractor: Melbro, Inc.
Photographer: Alan Holm

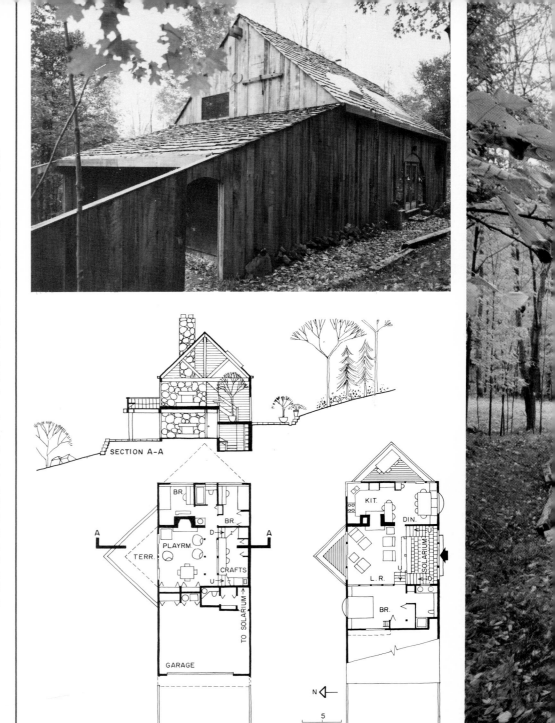

SECTION A-A

FIRST FLOOR

SECOND FLOOR

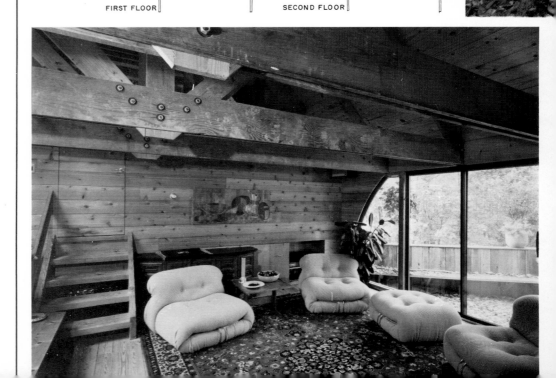

A small turn-of-the-century carriage house has been transformed by architects Crissman & Solomon into a study and laboratory for its owner—and can serve as a self-sufficient guest house. Within the small building the architects have created an environment of great distinction and warmth.

CRISSMAN HOUSE RENOVATION

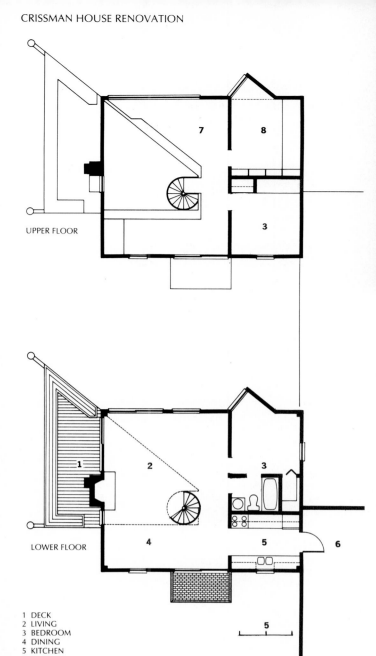

UPPER FLOOR

LOWER FLOOR

1 DECK
2 LIVING
3 BEDROOM
4 DINING
5 KITCHEN
6 BARN
7 READING GALLERY
8 STUDY

This renovated 60-year-old carriage house has been opened up to the west to afford its owners one of the most spectacular views in the greater Boston area. A very small building, only 25 by 30 feet, its lowest level is used as a garage and mechanical space. The main floor, which is at the same level as the barn floor with which it connects, has been transformed into a comfortable guest house with a living-dining area, a bedroom and a kitchen.

The second floor has become a mezzanine through the subtraction of a wedge-shaped portion. This judicious paring away adds to the volumetric complexity of the living-dining area, affording views upward to the roof and from the mezzanine downward to the main floor.

This solution was made practical by the existence of a solid wood beam, approximately 8 by 10 inches, which bisects the structure in the east-west direction and supports the second floor. It serves as the anchor for one end of the steel rod that became the necessary means of tying the south wall to the rest of the structure after the wedge-shaped portion of the floor had been removed. A vertical tie rod from which this beam is hung is part of the old structure and is connected to the trusses of the gambrel roof. Both the horizontal and vertical rods can be seen in the photographs opposite. The location of this beam determined the placement of the circular stair which ties into it at the second floor landing.

The old wood flooring which was removed was used for patching in the renovated areas. All the finished wood floors are made up of the old planks.

As the plans indicate, the south and west elevations were opened up as much as possible with the two-story living space and deck facing the view, and the smaller spaces arranged along the barn side of the building. The major view is captured from the study and the first floor bedroom by means of the angled windows which project from the west facade. The entire building was reclad in cedar shingles, except for the roof, which had been asphalt-shingled before the restoration. The cost without furniture was $20 per square foot.

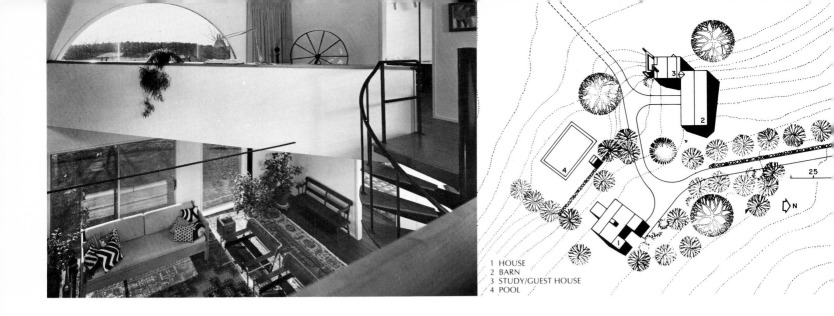

1 HOUSE
2 BARN
3 STUDY/GUEST HOUSE
4 POOL

The railing of the newly formed mezzanine is a continuous bookcase, which transforms the adjacent space into a reading gallery. The top of this bookcase serves as a useful ledge for plants and books and also provides reference space. Opening off the reading gallery is the owner's study with custom-built bookcases, files and a work ledge neatly fitted into the gambrel roof. From this study window the owner enjoys a magnificent view of the entire Boston skyline.

KIMBALL CARRIAGE HOUSE, Andover, Massachusetts. Owner: *Mr. and Mrs. John W. Kimball.* Architects: *Crissman & Solomon.* Structural engineer: *Eugene Hamilton.* Contractor: *Fitzgerald Henderson Porter Inc.*

Built just after the turn of the century, this carriage house was renovated for $85,000, a figure much less than the $250,000 that would be required, according to the architect, to build a similarly sized house today. The 100- by 40-foot house contains 7000 square feet, so on a cost per square foot basis, the remodeling is reasonably priced.

When purchased by the owners, the concrete block building was as it had always been—unfinished garage space. Architect Myron Goldfinger made minimal changes to the entrance façade (above, left), retaining the small 6-over-6 windows, and complementing the austere but mellow block walls with a simple, broad slab leading to the door. However, the large dormer roofed over in plastic suggests the light, contemporary interior (above photo, right) beyond.

Inside, the architect has opened the living space to a bedroom loft above, and to the outdoors by replacing old windows with three sliding glass doors. The cutaway section of the second floor permits a second-story dormer to light both floors, while affording a first-floor view of exposed timber trusses and tension rods.

The conversation area, formed by 9-foot-long built-in banquettes, achieves more height by being sunken. Conforming to the opening above, the banquettes provide an obvious separation of spaces, as well as storage.

The openness of the plan extends to the kitchen and pantry, separated from the dining area by a fireplace and two low counters with butcherblock tops. Lounging pillows on the floor in front of the fire pleasantly contrast—as do the exposed timbers—with the hard finishes generally used in the formal living and dining areas.

The first-floor gallery (see plan, page 20) retains the original brick floor, and wood and brass stalls of the former stable; the space is now used by the owners as a pottery studio.

PRIVATE RESIDENCE, Bedford, New York. Architect: *Myron Goldfinger*. General contractor: *John Allen*.

1978: $133,450 or $20/sq. ft.

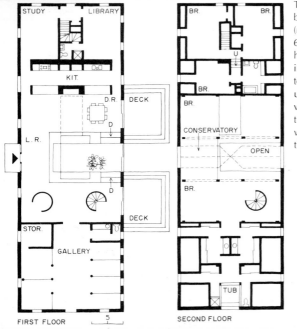

STUDY   LIBRARY

KIT.

D.R.   DECK

L.R.

D

STOR.

GALLERY

DECK

D

FIRST FLOOR   5

BR.   BR.

BR.

BR.

CONSERVATORY

OPEN

BR.

TUB

SECOND FLOOR

The attic loft became the master bedroom, with an adjacent bath (right) set into the hip roof. The 6- by 6-foot tub enclosure walls hide the toilet and shower, each in its own recess. The old elevator (above, extreme right) that used to lift the cars to the loft was retained as a piece of sculpture. A dormer window (above) was roofed in plastic to create the conservatory for plants.

"What's the use of living in the country if you never go inside and work on the garden?"

Chapter Eight:

BRINGING THE OUTDOORS INDOORS— AND VICE VERSA

Introduction

Houseplants have been with us since great-grand-mother's aspidistra, and even longer. We are tempted to speculate upon the relationship of the houseplant to the abrupt departure from the Garden of Eden — but architecture is inclusive enough without that kind of thing, so let's leave it at great-grandmother's aspidistra.

The houses chosen for this chapter have in common the inclusion of indoor gardens, usually benefiting from large glassed-in greenhouse areas, sometimes so thoroughly integrated that it is hard to tell where the house leaves off and garden begins.

In the Hall house (p. 128) we see a house so carefully fitted into its forest surroundings that it seems to have *grown* there rather than having been *built* there.

Still another response to nature is to provide decks, atriums, patios, and terraces to extend the living areas of the house to outside areas. While there is nothing novel in this approach — even developers build decks — you will notice that none of the decks or patio areas in these houses seem merely to be applied after the fact, stuck onto the houses as an afterthought.

On the contrary, the decks are careful parts of the over-all plan, integrating the surroundings into the plan. A very nice example of nearly all of these devices and effects can be seen in the Riley house (p. 126). There is an especially nice handling of the greenhouse and the deck here.

Another reason to cite the Riley house is its use of surplus solar heat collected in the greenhouse and stored for use during colder periods of the day. Supplementary heat provided by wood stoves is another adaptation made by the designer for this house in the woods.

Riley house
Guilford, Connecticut
Moore, Grover, Harper,
Architects

For this evergreen, stone-chocked New England site, architect Jefferson Riley designed his own house using traditional materials and time-honored building techniques. It is a tall house (four stories including basement) and it rises in a complex profile of setback and projection in each elevation. Dormers protrude from the sleepy pitched roof, adding to this sense of complication, and all exterior surfaces are richly mottled with shadow.

The south-facing gable end of the house is opened generously to the sun. The greenhouse below and the varied openings above fill the tall space behind with natural light and warmth. Surplus solar heat collected in the greenhouse is circulated along the insulated foundation wall and stored for radiation at night. The second and third floor bedrooms are set back from the exterior wall but open through windows to the tall space, thus taking advantage of light and view without additional heat loss. Supplementary heating is provided by wood stoves in the kitchen and living room. These stoves vent through the roof and the tall flues accent the verticality of the design.

The volumetric liveliness of the Riley house comes from the interplay of intimate spaces with the unexpectedly tall central space and additional fun is provided by unlooked-for details for double-hung windows on interior walls or a panelled wood door leading to the greenhouse.

Of his non-mainstream approach to design Riley says: "The house with its long gable roof, its double-hung windows, its red-stained clapboards, its central chimney, its over-all bilateral symmetry offset by asymmetrical parts, makes numerous allusions to colonial houses indigenous to its New England context. Yet we did not reproduce these traits by rote, but found joy in assembling them into a unique composition with contemporary strivings of its own."

Architect: Jefferson Riley
    Moore, Grover, Harper
    Essex, Connecticut
Contractor: Essex Builders
Photographer: Norman McGrath

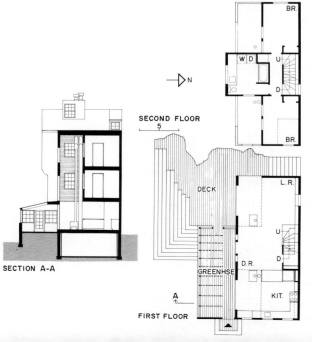

SECOND FLOOR

BR.

W D

U

D

BR.

N

SECTION A-A

DECK

L.R.

U

D

GREENHSE

D.R.

KIT.

A

FIRST FLOOR

Hall House
Napa, California
Roland-Miller, Architects

The owners asked for a small, year-round house that looked and felt like a vacation house. That is exactly what they got—and more. The site is a dramatic, six-acre hillside dropping down to a creek. Overhead is an almost complete canopy of tall redwoods. Making sensible use of the limited building space and dodging tree trunks with the utmost grace, the house stacks itself into two 20- by 20-foot units connected by a split-level stair (see plans overleaf). The uppermost level contains the master bedroom and bath as well as a private deck. The middle levels include living and dining spaces, kitchen, wrap-around deck and entry. The lowest level provides an additional bedroom and large recreation space. All these elements are brought together in plan and especially in section with really extraordinary sensitivity. Nowhere is there a sense that the site has been violated or that the plan is forced in its search for accommodation with these lovely surroundings. The surroundings, in fact, are keenly felt in every space through glass walls that provide only the merest hint of enclosure. Even the roof is opened in several places to provide occupants with views directly up into the towering treetops.

Finishes in the house are simple and appropriate: glass and exterior grade plywood for most wall surfaces; painted gypsum board inside. Structural bracing is added where needed over the glass. A mild climate, coupled with almost total shading from the vertical sun, makes the extensive use of glass practical. It remains pleasant and cool in the summer. In winter heating is provided mostly by wood stove and fireplace, supplemented occasionally with electric hot water and whatever radiated heat is furnished by a low-angle sun.

It is a splendid house, crafted to the site and the needs of its owner with exemplary success.

Architects: Roland/Miller Associates
   666 Seventh Street
   Santa Rosa, California
Owner: Clarence and Kay Hall
Contractor: Charles Gentry
Photographer: Barbeau Engh

1978: $30/sq. ft.

The interior spaces, though modest in scale, are exceptionally open and airy. The kitchen and dining area, (photos this page) feel almost uncontained. The bedroom (photo opposite) offers view in every direction—including toward the night sky—and the ladder leads to a small half hidden loft.

At about $30 p.s.f., the house was surprisingly inexpensive to construct.

ROLAND/MILLER

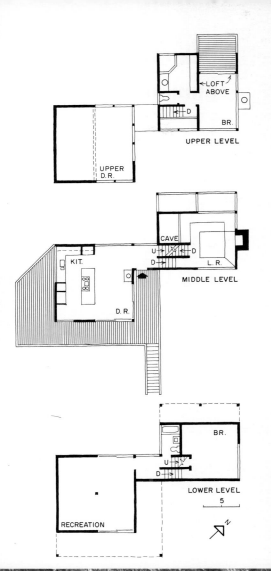

UPPER LEVEL

LOFT ABOVE

BR.

UPPER D.R.

CAVE.

KIT.

L.R.

D.R.

MIDDLE LEVEL

BR.

LOWER LEVEL

5

RECREATION

Hobbs Residence
Seattle, Washington
Hobbs Fukui Associates,
Architects

A steep, urban site sloping to the east with a view of woods, Lake Washington and the Cascade Mountain Range in the distance. Space for functions both common and private for two parents and three children. Architect Richard Hobbs brought these givens together in a l6-foot by 46-foot rectangular plan that distributes its functions over six interior levels. The entry level leads down to the children's areas or up to the main spaces of the house. Off these main spaces, and facing the view, is a narrow greenhouse that provides—in addition to a profusion of house plants—a fine sense of openness to the deck and woods beyond (photo below right).

Only from the downhill side does the verticality of the scheme reveal itself completely. From this vantage, the elaborately sculpted wood forms reach right to the tree tops giving the occupants of the upper levels a remarkable sense of privacy and an exhilarating feeling of elevation.

The interiors are carefully worked out and considerable spatial interest is achieved by powerful diagonal forms and by graceful circular projections into the main spaces. The extraordinary variety of openings also enriches the spaces, filling the interiors with daylight and broad streaks of sun that are especially welcome in the Northwest.

Heating is provided by a four zone system employing both electric baseboard and forced air units controlled from a central location. The principal finishes are cedar siding, anodized aluminum window frames, and gypsum board on ceilings and interior walls.

Architects: Hobbs Fukui
   150l Belmont Avenue
   Seattle, Washington
Owner: Richard Hobbs
Engineers:
   Robert G. Albrecht (structural)
   Neil H. Twelker (foundations)
   Martin/Datacom Associates (mechanical)
Interiors: Dallas E. Zeiger
Landscape: Thomas L. Berger
Contractor: Stole Building Co.
Photographer: Art Hupy

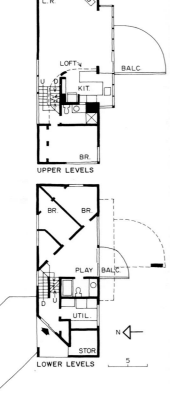

UPPER LEVELS

LOWER LEVELS

N

5

Architects: ERICKSON/MASSEY
  (Arthur Erickson)
Owners: Mr. and Mrs. William M. C. Lam
Location: Cotuit, Massachusetts
Job captain: Fred Dalla-Lana
Lighting: William M. C. Lam
Engineer: Bogue Babicki
Contractor: John B. Lebel

Landscaping, though still in the growth process, is as meticulously planned as the house. From the approach, the grounds dominate the simple facade, well screened for privacy.

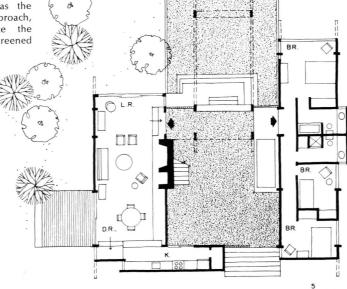

Phokion Karas photos

This summer home, designed for lighting consultant William M. C. Lam, gains an added cachet as the first U.S. project by architect Arthur Erickson of Vancouver—and therefore, the first of his houses eligible for a Record Houses award. Although not an expensive house (the cost was about $36,000), it has the same elegance, ease and power of the larger houses he has done in Canada. And, most important, owner Lam is pleased: "Unlike much of contemporary architecture, in which structure is displayed as a feature itself, Erickson's dramatic structures shape views, define spaces (rather than modules), and are a powerful yet subtle means of unifying complex combinations of spaces with numerous changes in levels. The quiet Cape shore views are given excitement when juxtaposed with the heavy framework of 6-by-16 rough fir beams and posts."

In a basic bi-nuclear scheme dividing living and sleeping spaces, the architect has used the post and beam framework to exuberantly link a variety of outdoor spaces with the interiors, and to carefully frame views in a manner reminiscent of classic Japanese architecture—of which Erickson is reportedly a great student. In a very interested student. In one (the enclosed spaces are tinted on the plan), but the close integration with outdoor living areas gives a sense of great spaciousness. There is also a detached guest house (not shown) with its own kitchenette, bath, deck and outdoor areas.

The exteriors and interiors have rough red cedar walls; the roof is built-up, floors are re-sawn fir, and partitions are drywall. With this as background, all the other interior finishes and furnishings are kept simple to reflect a summer house.

Court, gallery, terrace and deck form a succession of different outdoor living spaces. There is also a "project area and lower court"—a sheltered space below the bedroom block for rainy-day activities.

The living/dining room (above) is enlarged by planned vistas and decks. The kitchen is separated from the area by serving counters only, to increase the informal spaciousness; it also adjoins the central court.

A dramatic entrance stairwell—where fast growing trees and plants create an interior garden effect—is an ingenious solution to the problem of a steeply sloping site. At the same time, the stairwell provides an interesting focus for the main living areas. The device of a raised roof with a band of clerestory glass over the stairwell and dining area is skillfully employed to bring extra light and space into the center of a relatively small house. A handsome stand of eucalyptus trees flank one side of the site which can be glimpsed through these clerestory windows.

Of simple wood frame construction, this house—designed by the architect for himself and his family—makes substantial use of redwood for exterior and some interior walls and for the trellis (above left) which screens exposed glass areas from the sun and also gives shade to an outdoor deck.

1978: $59,800

The Woo House

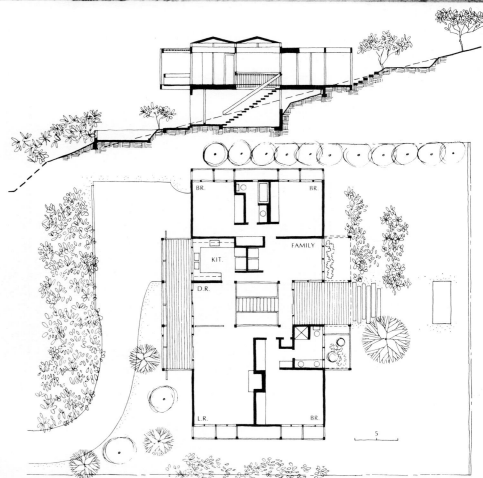

Some well-grown groups of trees on the southern and western sides of the lot protect the house from the heat of the late afternoon sun. An expansive view of the Los Angeles skyline is fully exploited by glass walls in the living-room, dining room and kitchen. A patio and terraced slopes at the rear of the lot make a pleasant playground for the two children, who can be easily supervised from the family room which overlooks this area.

Careful zoning allows plenty of living and entertaining space for the adults without conflicting with the children's activities. The children's bedrooms at one end of the house are separated by the kitchen and family room from the main living areas.

A carport and turning area have been cut into the hillside below the house and a steeply sloping driveway leads down to the street. The construction cost, exclusive of landscaping, was about $26,000 in 1966.

Architect and *owner:* Young Woo.
Location: Los Angeles, California.
Structural engineer: Tom Woodward.
Contractors: Colletta & Edgley.

Leland Lee photos

139

The low-budget house on a 50- by-100 foot suburban lot is a problem which many architects have faced. But few have solved it as smoothly as Donald Singer has here. The building lot, slightly longer but no wider than the panel, opposite, in which the plan is placed, dictated the linear scheme which in turn allowed concrete block masonry to be used in a remarkably straightforward way. This is an unusual degree of architectural unity for a low price.

But unity in this case does not mean simple plan geometry. Three distinct volumes interlock at the entrance to produce lively spatial sequences, different views from each room, extreme privacy and minimal circulation space. These virtues are achieved with construction economies that take into account the special problems of Florida building codes. Because of hurricanes, roof structures must be tied to a reinforced concrete beam at the top of all bearing walls which is itself directly connected to the footers (detail opposite, bottom). The nylon-asbestos roof surface also covers the fascias and eliminates possibility of roof-edge leakage completely.

Finally, the entire house is tied together by a single air-conditioning duct. This spine (detail opposite, bottom), requiring less than 50 feet of supply duct, also provides lowered ceilings in the passages which help define the dining room and which emphasize the living room.

1978: $45,240

Architect: DONALD SINGER, 1301 S. E. 2nd Court, Fort Lauderdale, Florida
Owners: Mr. and Mrs. Joseph Schmidt
Location: Coconut Grove, Florida
Engineers: Houha and Harry Associates
Lighting consultant: Edison Price
Interior design: Dennis Jenkins
Contractor: Henry Roloff

Joseph W. Molitor photos

GARDEN

BR.

SCREENED AREA

A — — A

L.R.

D.R.

LAUN.

BR.

BR.

PLAY

N   5

The living room (top right), dining room and master bedroom with enclosed garden (center), and children's playroom each have a different outdoor vista. Exterior views (opposite) emphasize the sculptural richness of house. Lettering on entrance continues inside, spells owner's name.

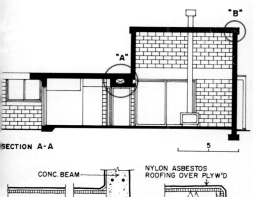

"B"

"A"

SECTION A-A   5

CONC. BEAM

NYLON ASBESTOS ROOFING OVER PLYW'D

WOOD JOISTS

REINF. BLOCK TIE BEAM

SCREEN VENT

WALLBOARD   AIR COND.

DETAIL "A"   DETAIL "B"

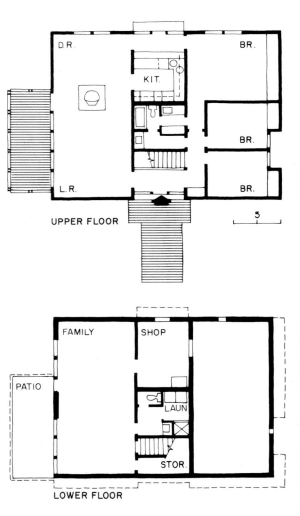

D.R.

KIT.

BR.

BR.

L.R.

BR.

UPPER FLOOR

5

FAMILY

SHOP

PATIO

LAUN

STOR.

LOWER FLOOR

The Glass House

Planned within the limits of a strict budget, this house was designed by the architect as a "first home" for himself, his wife and child—with planned expansion space for later additions to the family. Then (the house was built in 1963) an editor of *Better Homes and Gardens*, Frank Glass needed adequate working space and a pleasant environment for entertaining. The result is a simple, compact two-level dwelling which fits well into the sloping site and uses stock materials to their best advantage.

As the house faces a fairly busy residential street, the front elevation has been left completely closed. Large glass areas on the west and north side of the house provide good light and give a feeling of additional space. The main entrance is separated from the parking area by a wooden bridge.

Frank Glass says that this was done "in order to make the structure 'hang' among the tree limbs."

Although the total floor area of the house is only 1,500 square feet, clear-cut zoning gives considerable privacy to individual members of the family. Stairs connect the children's bedrooms on the upper level directly to the family room below and the play area outside. The kitchen, stair, bathroom and hall separate the entertaining area from the bedrooms. The well-placed entrance foyer, unusual in a house of this size, frees the living areas of general circulation. The cantilevered screened balcony on the west side of the house is shaded by overhanging trees, making a pleasant extension to the living room.

Architect and owner: Frank R. Glass. *Location:* Des Moines, Iowa. *Contractor:* Fritz Gookin.

Hedrich-Blessing photos

The Des Moines house is of post and beam construction on a concrete block foundation. Basement walls are of concrete block, painted where they are exposed. Plywood or glass panels in standard sizes were used for the rest of the exterior walls. Describing the exterior of the house, Frank Glass says: "The contrast of textures and the planned, rather formal balance of the exterior was achieved with stock materials. These materials, which required little cutting, were applied with careful detailing in pleasing proportions to give the house order." Exposed insulating deck is used for ceilings and floors and provides a base for the tar and gravel built-up roof. The photographs show how, inside the house, the dark posts supporting the ceiling beams form an effective contrast to the light-colored gypsum board wall panels.

The dining area is separated from the living room by a prefabricated fireplace, which rotates on its base to serve either end of the over-all room. A breakfast bar in the kitchen saves space and provides a convenient base for serving food to the dining room. The house is heated by a forced air system.

Weathered white cedar shingles and corner board windows are pure Cape Cod vernacular and picked because they make good sense. Decks (photo above) are off master bedroom; (below) off livingroom on second floor. Lower level bedroom windows peer through cedar trees close by. Entry leads to low-ceilinged hall (right), open to kitchen above, and yellow enameled cast iron spiral stair. Seemingly complex, the house was designed by juxtaposing two squares, then removing triangular volumes (for decks, pitched roof) as it goes up. House has concrete block foundation to anchor it to the ground, virtually composed of shifting sand.

When the owners leave their suburban home on summer weekends, they retreat to this unorthodox vacation house perched atop a Cape Cod hill. "Like a ship floating on the land" is how the architect Giovanni Pasanella's associate, Thea Kramer, describes the house, and the analogy is a good one. The hilltop site is flat, and, except for sand formations, scrub pines and other hardy flora, totally undistinguished. But the views—of the sea, a salt marsh, and a distant town—are great, and varied in all directions. No building is close by. By breaking up the usual four-square box to create many viewing angles (both through and out the house), the architect reasoned that he could take best advantage of the site, while still organizing the house for the owner's practical requirement: "an economical, varied space for themselves and guests to feel comfortable together or alone." The family includes a teenaged son and daughter, and separation of their activities was required.

Spaces and shapes lend this house its perennial vacation air of built-in delight and relaxation. It is a vacation environment—though equipped

1978: $47,790

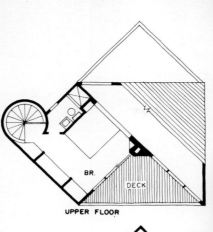

UPPER FLOOR

LOWER FLOOR

STOR.
BR.
BR.
BR.

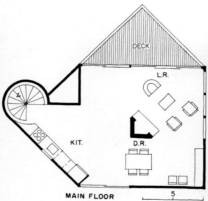

MAIN FLOOR

DECK
L.R.
KIT.
D.R.

5

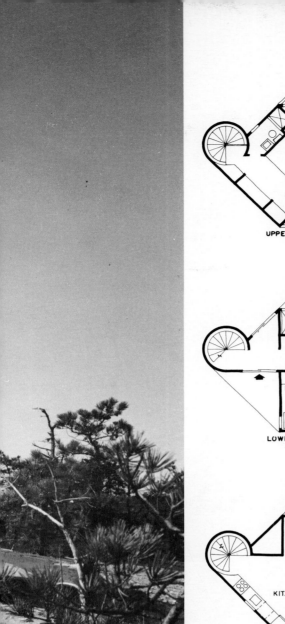

View (above) is master bedroom, overlooking livingroom and opening to its own deck, which, in turn, overlooks livingroom (below). Walls are cedar plywood; exposed structure is enameled a deep red. Exposed framing painted as trim helped account for total $27,000 cost. Play of space is stabilized by warm red tones and the orientation stair and fireplace provide.

David Hirsch photos

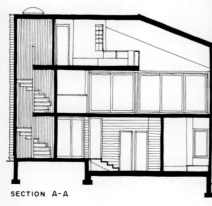

SECTION A-A

with space heating and all amenities for year-round use and planned with a realistic eye.

To take best advantage of the view, the usual multi-level house plan has been reversed, with major living areas open to major views on the second floor, and chil-

dren's and guest bedrooms a few steps below the first, or entry, floor. Master bedroom is on the third. By going up instead of out, and by placing main glass areas clear of the ground, the house can be totally buttoned up, and is worry free for the owners when away.

Architect: GIOVANNI PASANELLA
154 West 57th Street, New York City
Etel Thea Kramer, associate architect
Owners: Dr. and Mrs. Alan Grey
Location: Wellfleet, Massachusetts
Structural engineer: Stanley Gleit
Contractor: Allen Jordan

147

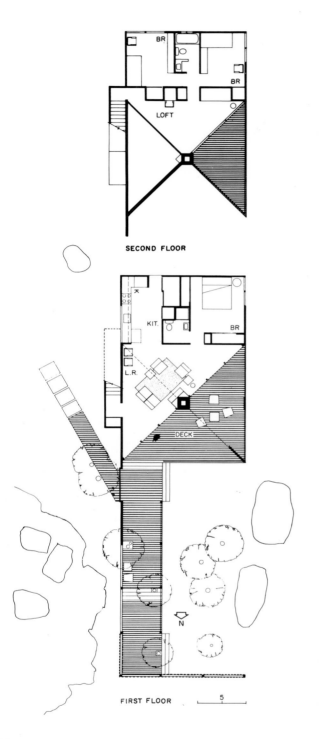

SECOND FLOOR

FIRST FLOOR   5

1978: $58,410

This year-round vacation home by architects Mayers & Schiff is located in the Pocono Mountains of Pennsylvania. The site is long and narrow with one end fronting on a pond. Part of the site— a small rocky ledge and a half dozen very large boulders strewn about—was high-ly picturesque but unsuitable for building on. The primary aim of the architects in siting the house was to incorporate this space into the design of the house itself. Approaching the house the first view is of a continuous sloping redwood wall which slices across the narrow dimension of the site and is punctured by a glossy white barn door. The wall hides all views of a pond and the large boulders, until the barn door is slid open—whereupon one is, quite unexpectedly, back outside! But not quite, for while part of the long wall forms one wall of the house, the

148

William Maris photos

The supergraphics of the Benenson house, designed by artist Florence Cassen, are an extension of the architects' basic diagonal concept. A continuous green stripe has been painted across the longest single wall surface (stairwell, below) in the house. A combination of sliding panels between the living room and

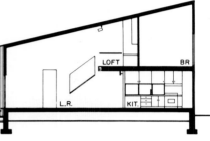

other ground floor spaces have also been painted with bands of varying widths. As panels are re-arranged in various ways, the stripes regroup to form new designs.

remainder is backed by a two-level open deck covered by a trellis. Both deck and trellis serve as wind bracing for this section of the wall. From the entry side one cannot tell where the house (the interior living spaces) ends and the long deck (one of the outdoor living spaces) behind

the wall begins; a fact that also intensifies the tie between the architecture and the natural spatial qualities of the site. At the point where the view of boulders on both sides, the cliff, and the whole natural setting is at its best, the wall is cut away, allowing nature to frame another type

of more open outdoor space. This area is the favorite outdoor sitting area for the residents. The unusual family makeup dictated special indoor space requirements: with four children varying from young ones still at home to older married ones who visit frequently, the Benen-

sons find themselves with an overflow crowd on some weekends and completely alone on others. Rather than build a large house with many bedrooms which would be "dead" space much of the time, the architects decided to limit the fixed bedrooms and provide a large sleeping

A variety of indoor and out-door spaces—and some that are not exactly either—provide the occupants of this Pennsylvania second home by architects Mayers & Schiff with living areas for every mood and weather change. The house has been carefully sited and de-signed not simply to sit in nor merely blend with its pleasant natural setting, but rather the most interesting features of the terrain have been integrated into the design of the house itself. This is achieved for the most part by the multi-level deck that extends the house into the woods, and by the partially roofed-over deck that brings the outdoors into the main structural volume. The design of the house is all the more impressive in view of the fact that little site work was necessary for the architect's goal to be accomplished. The house cost about $33,000.

loft with built-in bunk beds for guests. The sleeping loft, with its built-in work desk and adjacent outdoor deck, serves as a study for the Ben-ensons during the less-popu-lated weekends. The main form of the house is based on a square cut into overlapping triangles on various levels—a kind of tri-level tic-tac-toe—with a fireplace and chimney at the square's center. The long sliding glass wall of the triangular living room is ori-ented towards a view of the boulders and pond. The liv-ing room is two stories high in the space formed by the overlapping triangular loft.

Architects: ROBERT A. MAYERS and JOHN C. SCHIFF of Mayers & Schiff
Penthouse 45 East 51st Street, New York, New York
Owners: Dr. and Mrs. A. S. Benenson
Location: Hawley, Pennsylvania
Structural Engineer: Henry Gorlin
Mechanical Engineer: Seymour Berkowitz
Landscape Architects: Mayers & Schiff
Graphics: Florence Cassen
Contractor: Kreck-Myer

Chapter Nine:

IN THE CLASSIC MANNER

Introduction

While none of the houses in this book is a conscious or unconscious imitation of any given architect's work, the houses in this chapter crystallise many of the great themes in modern architecture. If these houses evoke memories of Frank Lloyd Wright, Mies van der Rohe or Louis Kahn, it is because of these great architects' influence upon the entire profession and practice of modern architecture.

It is interesting to note that Wright designed many houses for persons of limited means. His Usonian houses were fine examples of the master's art applied to the design of affordable houses.

There is, to be sure, a long tradition by which architects have, in the modern era, designed houses primarily for the truly affluent. But architecture is not a profession in which many grow rich, and of the houses in this volume, it is no accident that a healthy proportion are those designed by architects for that most particular — and unwealthy — patron, themselves.

Although at the time of writing architecture seems to be undergoing a change in which many of the cherished idioms of the International Style are being reevaluated it seems dubious that this will penetrate too far into the design of houses. House design by architects will probably continue to be a healthy blend of eclectic origins.

And so these houses, with a hint of Wright here, an echo of Mies there, represent a marvelous opportunity to summarize the content of this book, and to state emphatically that great houses are, and will continue to be, custom designed by architects for people like you and me — affordably so.

The Freidin House

An ample, sophisticated house has been achieved on a $30,000 budget (1967) by rigorous but discerning adherence to simplicity in design and materials.

The plan of the house is very straightforward: a long scheme places studio and guest room at one end of the house for quiet and privacy, family bedrooms at the other end, and living and service areas in the center. A slope in the site is utilized to provide the heater and utility room on a lower level under the west end of the house.

One of the things that gives the house its special character is its precision in the midst of a rambling, wooded setting. Jack Freidin describes its concept as a "house set on a recessed base so that it floats above the ground with controlled views of the surrounding woods. It is clearly separate and distinct from the ground —related to the site, yet not disturbing it. The use of fixed and sliding glass not only frames the view from each interior space, but relates that space with the site both visually and functionally." And one might add that, in spite of the compact, self-contained air of the design, the little recessed, outdoor decks by each of the glass walls provide a very positive and useful link with the grounds from most interior spaces.

The wood frame construction is also kept very simple. Roof joists, 24 feet long, span the width of the house, and are cantilevered, over dropped beams supported on posts every 14 feet. Posts are supported on the exterior foundation wall. The floor framing is the same as the roof, except joists rest on the concrete block foundation wall.

Architect and owner: Jack Freidin. *Location:* Weston, Connecticut. *Engineers:* Wiesenfeld & Leon. *Contractor:* William G. Major Construction Co.

An atmosphere of tidy, unaffected informality pervades the Freidin house. Most surfaces are natural-finish and easy to maintain. The exterior is sheathed with cypress siding. Concrete block used for the foundation is left exposed where the ground slopes to permit a lower level for a utility area.

Some areas of the cypress siding are carried inside as interior finish, but most walls and all ceilings are surfaced with gypsum board. Floors are oak, and have grills for the forced warm air heating.

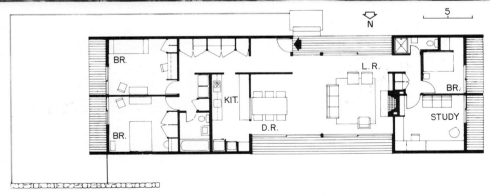

Marc Neuhof photos

The Grossman House

A tight budget and an open space program determined the design of this house built by Theodore Grossman for his wife and himself. Twenty-four-foot clear-span wood trusses support the floor and roof, opening up one large living space served by a utility core containing a kitchen, laundry and bathrooms. Core spaces are illuminated by skylights. The kitchen and the bathrooms are the only separate areas.

The house is located among pine trees and small rolling hills just east of the front range of the Rocky Mountains. Interior space is intended to relate to this natural setting and also provide a setting itself for objects and art works which the owners collected while they served as Peace Corps Volunteers in Colombia.

Sliding windows on the long sides are glass infill, permitting expression of the structural piers (all structure is wood); solid end-walls emphasize the direction of the trussed rafters.

Warm colors and materials soften the somewhat severe lines of the house. Siding is light-stained plywood with plank finish (left). Exterior decking is redwood; interior floor in the living space is oak. The front door is bright sky blue. Furnishings emphasize reds, whites, yellows, and black. Total cost in 1970, not including land and a well: $23,400.

Architect and *Owner:* Theodore A. Grossman, Jr., the TAG Associates. *Location:* Parker, Colorado. *Contractor:* Gerle Bros., Inc.

1978: $53,820

No doors separate the bedrooms and study from the rest of the interior, above. The wall around the study and large closet, right, does not reach the ceiling but serves as a non-structural screen from the living-dining area.

Rush McCoy photos

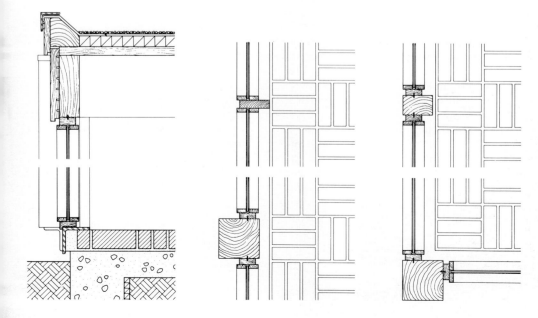

HICKMAN HOUSE

LAKESIDE MICHIGAN

Classic elegance in the Miesian tradition has been achieved in wood and glass for this restrained and finely detailed house in the country. Double virtues of sophistication and economy—the house cost $28,000—have been obtained through a modular coordination of structure and materials that is carried out in beautifully simple detail.

The structure is an exposed wood beam and column system of 24- by 6-foot bays. Plate glass walls and doors reaching from floor to ceiling are supported in wood framing. This rests on a continuous metal bracket that sets off the structure with quiet precision from its grassy site. The finished floor of brick, laid over a concrete slab on grade, is coordinated with the placement of columns and mullions, which alternate with the slender framing in orderly rhythm across the facade.

The site is a beautiful and romantic one—75-foot-high wooded bluff over looking Lake Michigan—and its seclusion offered an excellent opportunity of building a house with outer walls entirely of glass. The airy spaciousness of this glass pavilion is increased by an open plan.

The open, all-glass scheme is ideal for informal, country living—provided that the living be extremely tidy and civilized as well. To this end, the Hickman house neatly provides a clear separation of functions, ample storage space and unobtrusively placed utilities. These requirements are all satisfied by two interior partitions that flank the central living dining area. Behind one partition, the kitchen opens onto, but can be curtained from, a screen porch. The second hides neatly packaged bathrooms, water heater and storage; these double as visual and acoustical buffers, ensuring privacy for the two bedrooms at the far end.

Architect: David Haid, 108 North State Street, Chicago. Owners: Mr. and Mrs. F.W. Hickman; landscape architect: Paul Thomas.

1978: $57,680

Bill Engdahl, Hedrich-Blessing photos

The Sorey House

Seclusion and privacy are effectively combined with an expanded sense of space, created by open-plan, glassed-in living areas in this strong and forthright house. Although natural woods and heavy foliage help screen the site from surrounding suburban houses during the warm months, architect-owner Thomas Sorey, Jr., has carefully integrated story-high stone walls into the design to assure privacy to both indoor and outdoor living spaces. To contrast with all the openness below, the upper, bedroom floor is securely closed-in on the long sides by shingled exterior walls; this unbroken space is banked inside with a plethora of storage closets. All bedrooms have windows at the ends of the house, while the central (largely service) areas are skylighted.

The plan is well arranged for the family of parents and two small boys, and is devised to permit some changes in future years. For the present, the young children have an entrance via the utility room, where they can shed dirty or wet clothing and wash without tracking through the house; they also have access to the kitchen dining space without having to go through the major rooms when the parents are entertaining friends. The boys' bedrooms are primarily study-sleeping areas adjoining a skylighted playroom.

For later years, the boys' rooms have been built with non-load-bearing partitions which can be totally rearranged as needed. The master bedroom at the other end of the floor is quite large, and doubles as a sitting room; rough plumbing is provided in one of the closets for a future kitchenette so the children may "take over" the downstairs for parties when they are older.

Architect and *owner:* Thomas L. Sorey, Jr. *Location:* Oklahoma City. *Engineers:* Sorey Hill Binnicker. *Landscape architect:* William Warren Edwards. *Contractor:* Keith Hickox.

1978: $112,476

The Ernest House

An unusual amount of living space for a small, lower cost house was developed in this 1962 house by the architect for his own family. Three major design devices served to gain this goal: 1) a multi-level scheme minimizing roof and foundation area; 2) use of simple, low-cost materials—especially concrete block; 3) the placement of all utilities in a "service tower" to minimize piping, venting, etc.

The end result of these items, plus the placement of the stairs in a second "tower" to balance the service one, has been to free the interior for a number of open living spaces with a wide variety of sizes and views. As added height improved views of the ocean at the back of the site, and also gave better air circulation, major rooms were placed on higher levels, with the lowest floor devoted to stair entry, carport, workshop, and a laundry. The master bedroom, for example, has a clear view of the ocean across the upper portion of the porch.

As the lot is a long and narrow one, the side walls of the house were left blank, with no windows, for privacy from neighbors. The front and rear elevations are kept as open as possible for maximum light, air and view.

Architect and owner: Robert Ernest. *Location:* Atlantic Beach, Florida. *Structural Engineer:* Register & Cummings. *Contractor:* L. L. Abbott.

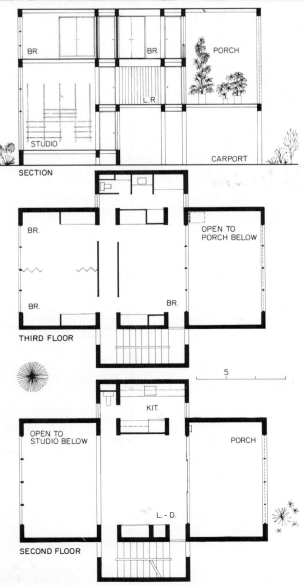

The structure of the Ernest house is principally of lightweight concrete block bearing walls, with concrete lintels and bond beams; roof and floor framing is wood. The "service towers" flanking the structure also serve as buttresses.

Finishes include clear silicone on the concrete block, gray stain and creosote treatment for wood. With the addition of some stained cypress walls, the interior walls are the same as the outside. Floors are wood covered with ship deck matting in living areas, sheet vinyl in the kitchen, and mosaic tile in the bath areas. All ceilings are wood with exposed beams.

Joseph W. Molitor photos

Abbott, Richard Owen 16-17
Adams House
    Roseau, MN 102-103
Arizona
    New River 24-25
Astle, Neil 32-33
BahrHanna Vermeer & Haecker 34-35
Baker, James B. 8-11
Baker and Blake 8-11
Ballentine House
    Atlantic Beach, FL 86-87
Barn 108
Benenson House
    Hawley, PA 148-151
Bohlin House
    West Cornwall, CA 28-31
Bohlin and Powell 28-31
Brandzel House
    Fremont, NE 34-35
British Columbia
    Vancouver 60-61
Bruder House
    New River, CA 24-25
Bruder, William P. 24-25
Burke House
    Watermill, Long Island, NY 22-23
California
    Berkeley 67-69
    Inverness 12-13
    Los Angeles 136-139
    Napa 128-131
    Plumas County 50-51
    Point Reyes 36-37
    San Diego 2-3
    San Francisco 18-19
    Sausalito 70-72
    Sea Ranch 40
Campbell House
    Sausalito, CA 70-72
Campbell, John Garden 70-72
Canavan House 64-66
Cannady House
    Houston, TX 6-7
Cannady, William T. 6-7

Carriage Houses 116-120
Cheng, James K.M. 60-61
Chimacoff/Peterson 80-81
Chiu House
    Vancouver, BC 60-61
Christiansen House
    Frog Hollow, MI 108-109
Colorado
    Denver 14-15
    Parker 156-157
Concrete block walls 4,88,140,165
Connecticut
    Guilford 126-127
    Westbrook 16-17
    West Cornwall 28-31
    Weston 154-155
Crissman & Solomon 116-119
Crossman House
    Sea Ranch, CA 40
Curry House
    Montauk, NY 104-105
Daland House
    Bethel, ME 52-53
Andrew Daland 52-53
Deck, cantilevered 45,53,96,137
Desberg House
    Central, OH 114-115
Design Consortium 112-113
de Swaan House
    Bridgehampton, NY 82-83
DeVido House
    East Hampton, NY 41-43
Devido, Alfred 41-43
Dunbar House
    Winhall, VT 46-49
Earnest House
    Atlantic Beach, FL 164-167
Earnest, Robert 164-167
Erickson/Massey 134-135
Florida
    Atlantic Beach 86-87,164-167
    Coconut Grove 140-141
    Miami 88-89
    Tampa 4-5

Index

Fowler House
    Houston, TX 73-75
Frankel House
    Margate, NJ 78-79
Freidin House
    Weston, CT......................... 154-155
Freidin, Jack 154-155
Glass House
    Des Moines, IA 142-145
Glass, Frank R. 142-145
Goldfinger, Myron 120-123
Grey House
    Wellfleet, MA 146-147
Grossman House
    Parker, CO 156-157
Grossman, Theodore A., Jr. 156-157
Gueron House
    East Hampton, NY 26-27
Gueron, Henri 26-27
Haid, David 158-161
Hall House
    Napa, CA 128-131
Heimsath, Clovis 73-75
Hickman House
    Lakeside, MI....................... 158-161
Hobbs House
    Seattle, WA 132-133
Hobbs, Fukui 132-133
Holmes House
    Tampa, FL 4-5
Holmes, Dwight...................... 4-5
Hunter, E.H. & M.K. 64-66
Illinois............................... 90-91
Industrial Materials 24,28
Iowa
    Des Moines 142-145
Kaplan, Richard D. 104-105
Karas House
    Berkeley, CA 67-69
Kimball House
    Andover, MA...................... 116-119
Kindorf House
    Plumas County, CA 50-51
Kindorf, Robert 50-51

Krueger, Paul H. 58-59
Lam House
    Cotuit, MA 134-135
Lamantia House
    Nyack, NY......................... 110-111
Lamantia, James R. 110-111
Larson, Thomas...................... 102-103
Leader House
    Sag Harbor, NY.................... 56-57
LeBovit House
    McLean, VA 100-101
Lipman House
    Denver, CO 14-15
Lot, narrow 2,4,16,70,78,94,104,140,148
Lovett House
    Crane Island, WA 44-45
Lovett, Wendell................... 98-99,44-45
Lowenstein House
    Montauk, NY 80-81
McKim House
    San Diego, CA 2-3
McKim, Paul W. 2-3
Maine
    Bethel 52-53
Mark House
    Truro, MA 58-59
Massachusetts
    Andover 116-119
    Cotuit 134-135
    Truro............................. 58-59
    Wellfleet 146-147
Maxey House
    Wayne County, PA 62-63
Mayers & Schiff 148-151
Meilleur House
    Bellevue, WA...................... 98-99
Metal cladding 24
Metal roofing 28,78,98
Michigan
    Frog Hollow 108-109
    Lakeside 158-161
Minnesota
    Roseau........................... 102-103
    St. Paul 112-113

Moger House
  Southhampton 84-85
Moger, Richard R. 84-85
Moore, Grover, Harper 126-127
Morgan, William 86-87
Nebraska
  Fremont 34-35
  Wausa 32-33
New Hampshire
  Hanover 64-66
New Jersey
  Margate 78-79
New York
  Annandale-on-Hudson 8-11
  Bedford 120-123
  Bridgehampton, Long Island 82-83
  East Hampton 26-27
  Montauk, Long Island 80-81
  Nyack 110-111
  Sag Harbor 56-57
  Southhampton, Long Island 84-85
  Watermill, Long Island 22-23
North Carolina
  Charlotte 96-97
Ohio 114-115
Oklahoma
  Oklahoma City 162-163
Opp House 112-113
Pasanella, Giovanni 46-49, 146-147
Pennsylvania
  Hawley 148-151
  Wayne County 62-63
Perry, Lyman S.A. 62-63
Plywood cladding 26,81
Poles, wood 16
Post and beam construction 2,12,32,63,86,134,142
Ream, James 14-15
Ream, Quinn & Associates 14-15
Riley House
  Guilford, CT 126-127
Riley House
  Inverness, CA 12-13
Riley, J. Alexander 12-13
Roland/Miller Associates 128-131
Rotner, Robert L. 22-23,56-57,82-83

Sandy, Donald, Jr. 40
Sauer, Louis Associates 78-79
Schmidt House
  Coconut Grove, FL 140-141
Schwarz House
  San Francisco, CA 18-19
Shafer House
  Annandale-on-Hudson, NY 8-11
Singer, Donald 88-89, 140-141
Sorey House
  Oklahoma City, OK 162-163
Sorey, Thomas L., Jr. 162-163
Stressed skin structure 36
Texas
  Houston 6-7, 73-75
Tigerman, Stanley 90-91, 108-109
Tollefson House
  Wausa, NE 32-33
Traverso House
  Eastbrook, CT 16-17
Trout Architects, Inc. 114-115
Van der Ryn House
  Point Reyes, CA 36-37
Van der Ryn, Sim 36-37
Vermont
  Winhall 46-49
Virginia
  McLean 100-101
Washington
  Bellevue 98-99
  Crane Island 44-45
  Seattle 132-133
Weinberger House
  Miami, FL 88-89
Weisbach, Gerald G. 18-19
Weisbach/Boutmy/Silver 18-19
Whisnant House
  Charlotte, NC 96-97
Whisnant, Murray 96-97
Wilkes, Joseph A. &
  Faulkner, Winthrop W. 100-101
Woo House
  Los Angeles, CA 136-139
Woo, Young 136-139